FAMILY LIVING IN PASTORAL PERSPECTIVE

LIVING
ALONE

HERBERT ANDERSON
AND FREDA A. GARDNER

WESTMINSTER JOHN KNOX PRESS
LOUISVILLE, KENTUCKY

Book design by Drew Stevens
Cover design by Jeff Tull, Fearless Designs

First edition

Published by Westminster John Knox Press
Louisville, Kentucky

This book is printed on acid-free paper that meets the American National Standards Institute Z39.48 standard. ⊗

PRINTED IN THE UNITED STATES OF AMERICA

97 98 99 00 01 02 03 04 05 06 — 10 9 8 7 6 5 4 3 2 1

Library of Congress Cataloging-in-Publication Data

Anderson, Herbert, 1936–
    Living alone / Herbert Anderson and Freda A. Gardner. — 1st ed.
        p.   cm. — (Family living in pastoral perspective)
    Includes bibliographical references.
    ISBN 0-664-25123-4 (alk. paper)
    1. Single people—Religious life.   2. Single people—Conduct of life.
3. Church work with single people.   I. Gardner, Freda A.
II. Title. III. Series: Anderson, Herbert, 1936–. Family living in pastoral perspective.
BV4596.S5A47   1997
248.8'4—dc20   96-36563

CONTENTS

INTRODUCTION

BLOCK PARTIES where I live in Chicago are testimony to the fact that people in Western industrialized societies live alone in increasing numbers. More than half of the sixteen units in my row of townhouses are single households. Some of the residents are divorced, others are widowed, one lives alone on the weekdays, two or three have lived alone all their lives, most are women. Not all communities will have so many single households. Since the last census in the United States, however, there has been a steady increase in the number of people who live in a household of one. Nearly one-fourth of all households in the United States are currently occupied by a single person.[1]

Many factors contribute to the rise of people living alone: longer life expectancy, the rising divorce rate, marrying later, greater affluence, all-consuming work schedules, growing privatization, increased urbanization, a diminished interest in having children or being responsible for them, and greater acceptance for being single. Cultural patterns are also changing—changing so that young people are more likely to live outside the home of their origin before they marry. Some people live alone because they want to keep their options open for personal development or satisfaction. Others live alone as a way of coping with stress in the workplace. Many people, however, do not choose to live alone. It simply happens. A pastoral response to living alone is necessary because it is happening more frequently.

Aim of the Book

This book is primarily about the experience of living alone at the end of a marriage—one way people come to live alone. In the sequence of the modern family's life cycle, one spouse usually dies first, leaving the other to live alone. The surviving spouse may eventually marry again or choose to live with a child or a friend, *but at some point for some time in almost every family's history, one spouse will live alone.* When one spouse dies, the surviving spouse will need to adjust to this new reality. Adult sons and daughters also have to make decisions about how to relate to the remaining parent. A family faces similar issues when parents divorce after the children have left home. Bette's story illustrates this inevitable dimension of the family life cycle.

> My husband died just before our fortieth wedding anniversary. We had a happy marriage. Because Don was in the military, we had moved eleven times during the marriage. I could not live where he died but I did not know where to live: with one of my five children? in the small Minnesota town were I grew up? near the nursing home where my mother lived? I chose a town where I had never lived before, near where my sister lived. It was the best decision I could have made. I learned to drive and write checks. I dyed my hair, got my first job, traveled to places *I* wanted to see, and eventually organized a home service for singles. I loved being married to Don but I often wonder what I would have become had he not died. (Bette)

Not everyone marries, however. *Some people live alone most of their adult lives.* We will consider their experience under the heading "always living alone." We are using "always" to mean that up to now and for the foreseeable future, one has lived alone and expects to continue living alone. Many people who have always lived alone thought they would marry. At some point, however, a person begins to identify himself or herself as someone who lives alone, acknowledges that "what is" may "always be," and understands that conclusion as an acceptable, even desirable life situation.

There are also a growing number of people who live alone temporarily or live alone while still being married. Some people view living alone after death or divorce as temporary because they expect to marry again. There are also married people who live alone temporarily because work, sickness, or imprisonment physically separates them from their partner. These "other circumstances" of living alone are increasingly common and raise pastoral and theological issues that churches must address. Everyone who lives alone, whether for a short or long period of time, must make sense of that reality in relation to the significant communities of their lives. We hope this book will help with that process of making sense of living alone.

— We intend this book for people for whom the death of a spouse or a divorce means that they live alone, not by choice but by the circumstances of their lives.
— We intend this book for people who realize retrospectively that they have always lived alone and are likely to live alone for the remainder of their life.
— We intend this book for people who experience their life as being lived alone in whatever context they live. We hope they will find validation of that experience in these pages.
— We intend this book for sons and daughters of aged parents who live alone, or nieces and nephews who have aunts and uncles living alone. We hope adult children will find help in understanding their parents who live alone and see ways of caring for them in order that they might grow old gracefully.
— We intend this book for church professionals whose ministry more and more involves relating to persons who live alone.

In one sense, everybody lives alone. The second book in this series, *Becoming Married,* suggests that a good marriage is one in which each person appoints his or her partner as guardian of the other's solitude.[2] If one aim of becoming married is to create a home in which one is free to have a room of one's own, in a sense we never stop being a single one. There is another sense, however, in which no one lives alone. Even the most fiercely independent people are connected to others in visible and invisible webs of love and obligation not always recognized. And if one's life is understood in relation to God's abiding presence as friend, then one is never alone.

Defining Living Alone

The definition of living alone used by census takers to determine the number of single households in this society is straightforward and objective. *Living alone means that the space one calls home is occupied by only one person.* To that definition we have added a subjective dimension. *Living alone also means to be without someone who is consistently involved in the ordinary and extraordinary decisions of daily living.* People who live alone are without the physical presence of another person with whom to share decision-making and the responsibility for place or style of living on an everyday basis. There are always many voices that inform our decisions, but for most of those who live alone, the final decider is oneself alone. We have chosen to emphasize the subjective experiences of living alone in order to broaden the sensitivities of church and culture.

—Living alone includes a widow with children nearby who are in and out of her home.
—Living alone includes a single, older man who has a companion he sees every day at work or at the senior citizens center or at dinner.
—Living alone includes a husband or wife whose spouse works in another place and from whom he or she is separated for weeks or months at a time.
—Living alone includes a recent college graduate who has a studio apartment in the same complex as her boyfriend.
—Living alone includes someone who has a single room in a retirement complex or a nursing home and eats some meals in a common dining room.

Living alone is not equivalent to being single. *People who live alone are ordinarily single, but not all people who are single live alone.* There are three other reasons why this book is not just about singleness. First, there are already a goodly number of books that address this question from various perspectives.[3] Second, living alone is both a subjective and an objective reality. Some recently widowed people who live alone do not as yet think about themselves as alone. People who are married may also live alone for a variety of reasons and for various lengths of time. Third, whether we live alone or with others, we are all "single ones." For that reason, maintaining the paradox of being separate selves in community is the same agenda whether one lives alone or lives with others.

Perceptions of Living Alone

Personal and social assumptions about living alone vary. Some regard it as a fulfilling lifestyle. In their book *Flying Solo,* family therapists Carol M. Anderson and Susan Stewart tell stories of women who have found being single and living alone to be a predominantly positive way to live.[4] Not everyone, however, has regarded living alone as an acceptable alternative to being married. In order to understand the ways people live alone with freedom and dignity, it may help to examine the cultural and theological reasons why it is regarded with suspicion. It is thought, for example, that people live alone because they are unwilling to share themselves or their possessions with others. Living alone is equated with being selfish or self-centered. Insofar as these perceptions continue, living alone remains a problematic thing. Because these attitudes continue in the culture, those who live alone are not surprised by negative perspectives on their life situation.

People are more likely to live alone in cultures that value independence or autonomy. There are many cultures in the world where it is neither socially acceptable nor financially possible for people to live alone. In that sense, this book is specific to Western cultures in general and North America in particular. And yet, as urban living spans the globe and people move away from villages and out of tribal communities, living alone is likely to become a more universal reality. Individualism is an increasingly global phenomenon. For that reason, the current communitarian impulse is an important voice on the other side because it keeps alive the fundamental human paradox of autonomy in community as an alternative to excessive individualism.

Living alone is not only a different experience for women and for men; there are different perceptions of its significance. There is an assumption, for example, continuing in our time, that men need to marry to be tamed. When the American colonies were being formed, it is said that William Penn assigned men to families where they could be supervised. A similar view is reflected in our time when some of the violence and instability of society is attributed to the increase of unattached males. Single men are regarded as problematic in society not only because they may procreate but not parent, but because they are not in family units that stabilize their behavior. The present promotion of marriage in this society is motivated in part by the desire to provide two parents for children. It is also aimed at socializing men. Certainly, being married has a settling effect on women and men alike. Promoting marriage as a permanent context for raising children and a relationship of mutual sharing and comfort between husband and wife should not, however, eliminate living alone as a responsible alternative—for men *or* women.

Even when it might be granted that people who live alone can be healthy, it is frequently assumed that they are not happy. We worry about friends who live alone, even when safety is not the primary issue. Parents do not wish their children to live alone. Even when people intentionally choose to live alone despite opportunities to live with others, it is difficult to imagine them happy. Yet such assumptions are not sufficiently paradoxical. The idea that people who live alone are not whole continues a vision for being human that is exclusively communal. Living alone and living with others in marriage or some other arrangement should be regarded as responsible ways of being human. We hope that the reader will discover in this volume positive alternatives to negative thinking about living alone.

Looking at Family from a Life Cycle Perspective

Each of the five volumes in this series on Family Living in Pastoral Perspective examines one of the changes that can be expected in the ordinary life cycle of a family: leaving home, becoming married, raising children, promising again, and living alone. The particular, intimate, often conflicted human crucible that we call the family begins to shape us even before birth. Our families hand us a legacy—their sense of what is right and wrong, their rituals, their peculiar rules—all with the same sense that these are not peculiar at all, but the universal rules by which human beings live. It is often a shock to discover that our family's way is only one of many ways, and that the way we thought was universal might not even be the best way. The legacy we have received from our families of origin is the first and most powerful resource we have to help us negotiate the transitions and changes that mark our family's history.

The family as a social system changes according to its own history of evolving tasks. Each major transition in its life cycle offers a family the possibility to become something new. Such moments of transition create a crisis in the ordinary sense of that word because they are turning points at which things will either get better or worse. It is not possible to have change without crisis or without grief. A family's capacity to grieve its anticipated as well as its unanticipated losses will in large measure determine its ability to live through the crises of change. If marriage preparation, for example, ignores the changes and contradictions in becoming married that evoke grief and sadness, it will impede rather than enhance the possibility that God is doing a new thing in forming this new family.

The family life cycle perspective is the most practical and effective way of helping people understand the family as a social unit with a life and history of its own. It also provides a framework for thinking about how ordinary pastoral interventions related to the church's ritual life correspond to critical moments of transition in the family's history. The church's ministry with families often requires a delicate balance between attending to the needs of individual children and adults throughout their stages of development and attending to the needs of the family as a whole as it experiences change.

There are two ways to link this book with the rest of the series. When one spouse dies or when couples divorce near the end of a family's life cycle, learning to live alone is the last task in a series of family tasks. These tasks include leaving home, becoming married, raising children, promising again, and finally, living alone. For people who remain single and do not raise children, the idea of living alone must be thought about in new ways at each significant moment in the history of *an individual's life cycle*. Living alone may also be the life task if a marriage ends by divorce or the death of a spouse when there have been no children. Living alone may occur when the last child leaves the home of a single parent. It is the life task when a spouse dies or the marriage ends in middle years after children have left home.

The loss of a spouse is a crisis for the entire family. When that loss occurs at the end of life, the family as a whole may lose its organizing center ("Mom was the one who brought us together") or its financial base ("My father was always willing to help us out in a pinch") or emotional presence ("Christmas was not the same for our children after grandpa died"). As parents live longer, the burdens for middle-aged sons and daughters will increase. An aged parent who insists on living alone may still require daily attention from an adult child who is retired. When the loss of a spouse occurs because of divorce, the issues in relation to family of origin are more complex. It is not clear how families are to respond to a former in-law who, for instance, wants to keep in touch with the grandparents of his or her children. When parents assume that a divorcing daughter or son will come to live with them, one might conclude with some certainty that the divorce has something to do with incomplete separation from the home of origin.

The Paradox of Family Living

Throughout this series, we have attempted to keep in paradoxical tension several seemingly contradictory statements about living in families that relate to the fundamental human paradox of autonomy in community. The paradox of communal autonomy implies two distinct convictions about human life that seem to be in contradiction. Each individual is to be honored as an autonomous creation of God with particular gifts to be developed and exercised *and* each individual is a communal being whose individual uniqueness and ultimate destiny is formed in relation to others and for the sake of others. The understanding of Christian anthropology that undergirds this book (and the entire series) seeks to maintain communal autonomy as a central paradox for human wholeness.

Contradictions that are true are not accidental. They are inherent in human nature, in the circumstances of our lives, and in the dynamics of family living. In a book titled *The Age of Paradox,* Charles Handy has observed that paradox is like the weather: something to be lived with, not solved. "Paradox has to be *accepted,* coped with and made sense of, in life, in work, in the community, and among nations."[5] Living with paradox need not confuse us even though it will often surprise us. Balancing the contradictions of family living is therefore neither random or haphazard. It is a way of remaining faithful to a view of human nature that is paradoxical enough to be consistent with experiences of life and major themes in the Christian tradition.

The struggle to keep this paradox in balance varies throughout the life cycle of a family. The leaving-home process often exaggerates autonomy in order to enhance the likelihood of forming a separate and distinct self. Philosopher Raymond A. Belliotti has observed that there is no escape from this autonomy-community continuum. "Humans must distance themselves from their families, at distinct times and to various degrees, to actualize fully their potential."[6] The process of becoming married is a delicate, paradoxical dance in which two people seek to form a home in which both partners have time and space of their own. That same need to keep balanced the paradox of community with autonomy is replayed when the nest empties.

This paradox of family living is, as Belliotti suggests, at the heart of human experience. "We simultaneously long for emotional attachment and are horrified that our individuality may evaporate once we achieve it."[7] Living alone presents the same dialectic that exists for people who are married: keeping the balance between honoring separateness and honoring togetherness. People who live alone are sometimes regarded as incomplete. The theological and pastoral task is to understand the nature of human nature in such a way that one can actualize that paradox while living alone as well as when living with others.

If change is central to the vitality of a family's life over time, paradox is what gives shape to its meaning and sustains its well-being in time. Paradox remains even when change occurs. Families are likely to get in trouble when they do not keep alive both dimensions of the paradox. So are individuals who live alone. Because people would rather stand on one side of a paradox or the other, our ministry with families and individuals requires that we intensify these creative tensions by "saying the other side." In the previous books in this series, this phrase "saying the other side" has been identified with a variety of pastoral strategies, all having as their purpose living with paradox.

It is our pastoral task to intend paradox precisely because the unresolvable contradictions in our lives often become the occasion for transformation. And if transformation is to occur, there can be no room for absolutizing. Faithful and vital living as families and individuals begins with the conviction that *there is another side*. "Saying the other side" is a way of making sure that everyone's voice is heard. This is a liberating pastoral method if each side of any paradox is respected *and* if everyone agrees that the deepest truths of life and faith are to be found in paradox. Then the helper's task is to assist people to live in the paradoxes of existence that are central to individual and family well-being throughout the cycles of life.

A Practical Theology for Ministry

Each of the first four volumes in this series has included reflection on the implications of a particular life cycle crisis for some aspect of the church's ministry. *Leaving Home* included some discussion of the pastoral care needs of daughters and sons leaving home and parents left behind. In *Becoming Married*, the emphasis was primarily on ritual. Planning a "wedding that weds" is one way to take seriously the process of becoming married. The ministerial emphasis in *Regarding Children* was both organizational and catechetical. The public commitment of a congregation to become a "sanctuary for childhood" also implies a willingness to make explicit, through its preaching and teaching, that the church is a place of safety for children and childhood. The work of *Promising Again* linked care and ritual in the ministry of a congregation with couples at significant transitions in the history of a marriage.

The aim of this book is to explore all aspects of the church's ministry with people who live alone and to understand that ministry in the light of the entire ministry of a particular gathered people of God. The church's ministry begins with a recognition of the diversity of living situations for people today. The practice of "saying the other side" is one way to understand a ministry that supports both living alone and living with others as responsible alternatives. In the concluding chapter, we will use practical theology as a framework for linking pastoral care, preaching, worship, and religious education around ministry with those who live alone.

Martin Marty wrote in a book titled *Friendship* that "you can kill people with a gun and you can kill them with an apartment."[8] The truth of this statement became very evident in Chicago during the summer of 1995 when over five hundred died from heat-related causes. A large percentage of those who died lived alone in one-room apartments around the city. They were all alone with no one to look out for them. Most of them died because they were isolated, afraid, and alone. If there is some sense of urgency in this book as we address the questions about living alone in the church and in society, it is probably because most of it was written during that tragic summer of lonely death.

Acknowledgments

This series on Family Living in Pastoral Perspective is the outcome of years of collaboration with Kenneth R. Mitchell. Unfortunately, Ken died suddenly of a heart attack on February 18, 1991, before this project could be completed. Although this volume has been written with Freda Gardner, the spirit of Kenneth Mitchell is very much present. I am very grateful to the friends (new and old) who have joined with me in completing this endeavor: *Becoming Married* with Robert Cotton Fite, *Regarding Children* with Susan B. W. Johnson, and *Promising Again* with David Hogue and Marie McCarthy, S.P. The collaboration with each of these authors has enriched the project as a whole. Conversations that occurred among the authors and spouses during the writing of the epilogue were invigorating, challenging, and further confirmation that the themes in this series continue to have relevancy for the future of family.

During the time these volumes have been written, I have also been involved in the "Religion, Culture, and the Family" project sponsored by the Lilly Endowment and directed by Don S. Browning. While the themes under consideration for that project are not directly related to this series, I have been personally stimulated by that ongoing conversation in ways that have enriched the writing of this series, Family Living in Pastoral Perspective. My thanks also to the editors and staff of Westminster John Knox Press who have shepherded this series to its conclusion.

Freda and I are grateful to many people who have read some or all of this manuscript and offered helpful criticism and significant insights as this project has evolved: Phyllis Anderson, Terry Burke, Linda D. Even, Roy Hoffman, Susan B. W. Johnson, Connie Kleingartner, Steven Kerschner, John Linnan, C.S.V., Patti Luebben, Judy Mitchell, Marilyn Olson, Virginia Piecuch, and Karen Speerstra. We are also indebted to many people who have told us their stories about living alone personally or through a questionnaire. While the stories have been altered to preserve their anonymity and their real names do not appear, these people have been internal partners with us in writing this volume. The stories ascribed to Herbert or Freda are, however, the actual stories of the authors. When Kenneth Mitchell and I began this project, I had in mind that the story of Freda Gardner, as someone who lives alone with faithfulness and integrity, would find its way into the book. It is a gift to me that she is now the coauthor of the final book in the series.

HERBERT ANDERSON

Easter 1996

1

LIVING ALONE,
BEING WHOLE

WHETHER WE live alone or live with others in marriage or some other form of community, one question is the same: How do we keep a balance between autonomy and community, between being separate and being together? For people who live with others, honoring their identity, developing their own unique gifts, and preserving time for solitude in the midst of community is sometimes a struggle. Those who live alone, on the other hand, need to balance their solitary time by participating with others in ways that enhance their being a communal person. The paradoxical reality of communal autonomy is valid both for those who live alone and for those who are married. Only the starting point changes.

> I was meeting with some young women to plan a church group for mothers with young children. The living room of the home where we met was filled with two playpens, two jump seats, and the random movement of several toddlers. As the meeting was ending, I said I had to leave for a luncheon appointment. I was surprised and puzzled by their response. More than one woman said something like "it must be wonderful to do things like go to lunch and not be bound by a family schedule." In response, I said, "while you are envying me, I look at a room full of paraphernalia and children and I think how wonderful such a life must be."   (Freda)

How we think about the paradox of communal autonomy depends in part on our starting place. Freda's story reveals the common human tendency to judge another's life as more desirable than one's own. In a deeper sense, however, the story points to an ongoing human dilemma: *If we live alone, we may long for community, but when we live with others, we long for time alone.* The human struggle for a balance between being alone and being with others never seems to end. The demands of professional life often diminish the capacity to be emotionally available or even just good company to another person. When one spouse dies at the end of a family life cycle, this struggle continues even though it takes a different turn. The same people who envied the freedom of people who live alone may now also judge that way of living to be less than satisfying or normal. As a result, people who live alone are sent the same message in a variety of ways: It is not good to live alone.

It Is Not Good to Live Alone

In this society, in churches, in one's family, even among friends, those who live alone may be well-loved and envied but they are also pitied, sometimes feared, and frequently perceived as self-centered. Because people who live alone are part of the same society, church, or family that fosters these negative responses, they often share this mixture of attitudes and values about the way they live. We do not intend this book to add to the spoken or silent judgment of living alone. Rather, our aim is to examine in a compassionate manner the struggles that people face as they seek to live alone responsibly and with joy. In subsequent chapters we will explore, in a more focused way, (a) living alone after living with another, (b) living alone for all or the greater part of one's adult life, and (c) living alone on a temporary basis. In this chapter, however, we ask about the normative question beneath our silent judgments: Is it good to live alone?

> They don't all say it the same way, but to me the message is the same: People who live alone are incomplete. Sometimes it seems like they assume I am superficial or selfish because I live alone. Even though there are more of us today who live alone, it is still an uphill struggle not to feel diminished. One day I am pitied; the next day someone admires my courage to "live the way I live." At a family wedding recently, I was seated with second cousins in their teens and early twenties. At forty-four, I still never sit with couples. Apparently, they have decided I am not grown up yet. (Dennis)

Unfortunately, the story Dennis tells is all too common. Moreover, it is seldom limited to the never married. Although the story does not say it, Dennis was divorced. Widows and widowers have told us similar stories. Whether people who live alone are admired or judged, one enduring assumption is that the world was meant to be coupled. Human beings are created as women and men, suggests theologian Letty Russell, so that we would be "not lonesome but twosome."[1] From this perspective, life with others is not only an antidote to loneliness—it is the norm for human wholeness.

However one comes to live alone, whether it occurs at the end of a life when one spouse dies leaving the other to live alone, or because of divorce, or after caring for an aging parent, or whether it happens that one lives alone from the beginning of one's adult life, the existential question is the same: *Can I live alone and be whole?* This question is both new and old. It is an old question formed by philosophical and theological views on human nature. It is new because single households are increasing. Even though the number of people living alone continues to increase, it is still regarded as a deviation from the norm for human living.

> My grandmother used to say, whenever she felt the need to explain an improbable marriage, "God made them and matched them." I think now she meant to say something about the mystery of God and maybe even the mysterious way in which people choose or are chosen in marriage. When I felt bold, I would say out loud to grandmother what I often thought, whenever she offered her simple wisdom, "If God made a match for me, when will that match be found?" Grandma had no answer. Now, thirty years later, when someone calls and asks if my husband is at home, I sometimes say, "No, he's never home," as I visualize some poor lost soul still out there looking for me, looking for the match God made. (Freda)

Freda's grandmother was clear about her norm for human living. Her answer to the existential question about whether one can live alone and be whole would be no. The world was made for couples; God made them and God matched them. Since grandmother's generation, however, living alone has become more socially acceptable, more financially possible, and sometimes even professionally necessary. Therefore, we need to continue to ask whether and how it is possible to live alone and still be whole and faithful to a vision of Christian living. We expect to give an affirmative response to the question. We regard diverse patterns of living alone and living with others as instances of the extravagance of God's creation.

In the same way that it is possible to live faithfully as a Christian in a variety of family structures, so also we believe it is possible to be a whole, faithful follower of Christ and live alone or live with others in marriage or some other form of human community. We intend to examine questions about living alone from several perspectives (developmental, cultural, biblical, and theological) in order to deepen our understanding of both the question and our response. We begin with developmental issues related to living alone not because they are most important but because they connect most immediately to our experience and to the life cycle perspective of this series on family living. Moreover, most people who live alone are still part of a larger family unit to which they continue to relate.

Developmental Perspectives on Living Alone

Leaving home is a natural, necessary, and promising task that carries some of the same risks of earlier developmental tasks. The risk that the young child takes in saying "no," that the school-age child takes who begins to not tell everything to the parent, that the teenager takes who is critical of parental values and family mores, and that the adult son or daughter takes who disappoints parental expectations by living alone is the same: Everything that is dependable and essential may be lost. Finding one's own identity, establishing one's autonomy, becoming independent of being defined by others is particularly the work of the adolescent and young adult years, but it may continue as "work yet to be done" well into adulthood, and, for some, throughout life.

> I knew who I was when I was Jane's husband and the children's father but now that she is gone and the children are no longer a regular part of my life, I sometimes wonder who I am. I don't even have my job to tell me at least for some hours of the day that I am Mr. Laurentzen.   (Peter)

To people who knew him, Peter seemed clear about who he was and what he did. At a more fundamental level, however, he had depended on Jane to provide him with a sense of self. When she died, he was bereft and his friends were puzzled. It turned out Peter was a seemingly independent person who had depended on his wife to establish and maintain his identity in the world. Having to live alone after living with someone who fashioned one's sense of self generates a crisis of identity that complicates the process of coming to terms with living alone.

Each of us works at the developmental task of individuating from our homes of origin with varying degrees of success. In order to establish one's identity, adult daughters and sons must break away from those who have, until that point, provided identity and the security of belonging to a family. An individual who has not accomplished this task of leaving home is less likely to enter new relationships or live alone with a fully formed self. Whether this process of separating is the same or even as necessary for women as it is for men is a topic for future discussion. In any case, a family must often change its perception of adult children who leave home and live alone.

> The unspoken definition of adulthood in our family includes being married. I am not. My parents have more to say about how I live and carry out my personal life and my professional work as a pastor than they do about the way my brother lives. Furthermore, my choices are frequently challenged. My brother's are not. Even though I am the oldest, my parents ask my brother when they are looking for advice about their retirement, health care, or wills. When I visited my parents after Christmas last year, they consulted my brother about where to hold a special family dinner. It has always been a rule in our family that adults are consulted but children are informed. Since I have not achieved adult status through marriage, I am not consulted.   (Evelyn)

Evelyn's story suggests that if being married defines adulthood, parents are likely to regard their children who are single and live alone as less than whole. There are other factors that also need to be kept in view as one explores the developmental issues for an adult living alone: issues of living as they are experienced by the person living alone; the response of other family members to the individual over time; how the developmental stages of other family members affect the way the single adult deals with not marrying; and how the family as a whole needs to rethink its self-definition. People like Evelyn often experience tension with their families when their own growth in self-understanding and self-acceptance is not matched by parallel changes in the perception of their homes of origin.

Those who enter adulthood fearful that their individuality will vanish if they achieve emotional attachment will be cautious about living with others. People who "end up" living alone may have a clearly defined sense of self but may not trust that sense of self to endure the pressures of living with another. For such people, independence becomes a substitute for autonomy. There are others who use intimacy with another person as a way of establishing an identity. Without that other in relation to whom and against whom an identity has been forged and maintained, a widowed or divorced person may flounder and become confused. Ideally, personal identity is influenced by, but does not depend on, those with whom we live.

My mother died a year ago, in an auto accident in which my Dad, seventy-seven, was the driver. My Dad loved my mother dearly, so I tend to believe that there was not much ambivalence on his part about the relationship. It is clear that he had an identity quite separate from his relationship to my mother. I attribute some of this to the fact that Dad grew up on a farm with six brothers and one sister in addition to hardworking parents in a materially poor, dust bowl, depression-era home in Colorado. I believe he had to be differentiated in that time and context in order to survive. Today, he lives alone and seems to be thriving.

(Bernard)

The developmental task for Bernard's father is the same for everyone: to establish a sense of self that is autonomous enough to welcome intimacy and community without fear of absorption or the loss of freedom. Those who live with others are challenged regularly not to confuse dependency with intimacy. When it has been difficult to differentiate from the claims of family, those who live alone need to be watchful that independence not become a substitute for autonomy. Independence has a place in human interaction when it is used to strengthen human community or in service to the common good. Moreover, the spirit of independence often reflects, in the lives of those who live alone contributes vitality, energy for the diversity of gifts to interdependent contexts. Differentiating intimacy, for the sake of intimacy, is developmentally normative for the community of ...kind that God is creating.

Cultural Perspectives on Living Alone

The Western conception of the person as a uniquely defined self, functionally disconnected from community, is not the dominant view of being human in the context of the world's cultures. The concept of an autonomous individual, free to choose and free to live alone, is an alien, even troubling idea to people from most cultures because it seems to doom an individual to a life of isolation and loneliness. For most people of the world, the identity of an individual is not separated from the identity of the tribe, clan, family, or some other larger social grouping. In cultures that are communal or sociocentric more than individualistic or egocentric, the end of human development is adulthood and interdependency.

The way to achieve adult status varies across cultures. There are still cultures for which becoming married is the only road to adulthood and full humanity. The absence or delay of marriage is cause of concern when marriage is the ultimate criterion for adulthood. The expectation that children should remain in their home of origin until they marry is being challenged, however, by new criteria for leaving home. When marriage is considered the natural transition to adulthood, the move from living in one's home of origin to living alone causes conflict and hurt because it is interpreted as an act of disloyalty, bringing shame to one's family of origin.

In a comprehensive study titled *Leaving Home before Marriage*, sociologists Frances K. Goldscheider and Calvin Goldscheider conclude that separation from parents, not marriage, marks the end of childhood. "Nonfamily residential autonomy has become normative in the transition to adulthood: it is expected and experienced by a majority of young adults."[2] Adulthood is increasingly defined as the ability to support oneself. What the Goldscheiders have defined as "nonfamily residential autonomy" is a technical term for living alone, and it has become the normal road to adulthood.

Richard Shweder has developed a psychological perspective ("cultural psychology") that recognizes diverse ways of being human because of the reciprocity between the individual and his or her culture. Culture and psyche, person and context, self and the other, Shweder maintains, create each other. As a result, there are various ways of understanding what it means to be human. "There are no universally or uniformly valid requirements for what languages to speak or what foods to eat or what clothes to wear and so on."[3] Nor, we would add, is there a universal standard prescribing living alone or living with others. Patterns of living emerge from the intentionality of both individual persons and their cultural worlds. Thus, in social interaction and in social practice, "the intentionality of a person meets the intentionality of a world and they jointly facilitate, express, repress, stabilize, transform, and defend each other through and throughout the life of a person or the life of a world."[4] If Shweder is correct, diversity of life patterns is to be expected within and across cultures.

The focus on the individual as an autonomous and uniquely defined self is a necessary mark of adulthood, but it is an inadequate view of being human. It is also an insufficient criteria for judging human wholeness. Human well-being and fulfillment are ultimately communal. The basic irreducible unit of humanness, according to David Augsburger, is "person-with-relationship-to-significant others."[5] Most but not all of those relationships are sustained by living together. And living in family is the dominant pattern of being together. It is possible, however, to live alone and be whole even in sociocentric cultures as long as one continues to develop ways to foster communal integrity as well as individual identity.

Biblical Perspectives on Living Alone

According to Phyllis Trible, the creation narratives in Genesis are clear about one thing regarding being human: "The earth creature needs a companion, one who is neither subordinate nor superior, one who alleviates isolation through identity."[6] *It is not good for the human one to be alone.* Beyond that, there are a wide variety of interpretations of the creation of humankind. We presume that these creation narratives provide a view of coequal creation and coequal responsibility of woman and man. We hold, moreover, that the human person is defined primarily in relation to God, who is represented by images of both sexes. As such, the creation stories in both Genesis 1 and Genesis 2 are about theology and anthropology more than cosmology.

The human story begins with forming a relationship. Being in community is the central characteristic of being human. That the human creature was formed from the dust is yet another metaphor for the interdependence of all life in creation. The human creature "who has been taken from the ground will in turn work the ground that has been watered by God."[7] For Old Testament theologian Dianne Bergant, this shows both human interdependence with the earth and the affinity between the human beings and other earth creatures. In fact, the reason for the creation of other animals was so that the human creature would not be alone. "Then the Lord God said, 'It is not good that the man should be alone; I will make a helper as his partner'" (Gen. 2:18).

In this creation account, God made woman because no animal was an adequate source of companionship and because it was not good for the man to be alone. The word *alone* comes from a Hebrew verb that means to separate or divide, and therefore suggests more the idea of being incomplete rather than being "by oneself." "It is not good that man remain incomplete, and so God will make someone like this man who will act as a mediator of blessing for him."[8] The human creature is not only interdependent with all creation but also incomplete without a suitable partnership.

The biblical description of the creation of humankind in Genesis 2 is often interpreted as a mandate for marriage as we know it. As the writer of Genesis 2 tells the story, the institution of marriage is the logical extension of creating woman as a remedy for man's aloneness. What is clear from the writer in Genesis 2 is that humankind is male and female, equal and distinct. And there is no full humanity without both male and female together. The marriage bond of equal partners is intended to meet our deepest needs for relationship. Even though some marriages today may intensify rather than alleviate loneliness, the promise of the "other" remains a sign of God's merciful kindness. We are not meant to be alone.

Letty Russell has made an interesting observation about the Genesis stories that expands the possibilities for human living as communal beings. Man and woman are created as sexual beings for the purpose of community and companionship, not just for procreation. Human sexuality refers to a whole range of behaviors that go into our makeup as male and female.[9] Sexuality may be expressed through sexual intercourse, but it encompasses much more than that. We understand that human beings are not meant to *be* alone even though some *live* alone. The dominant biblical message is that human beings are meant for community. Marriage and family has been, and will continue to be, the most common expression of that impulse toward community. Even from the biblical perspective, however, the question of human wholeness is settled not by "whom we live with" but by "the way we live." Compassion, justice, faithfulness, forgiveness, and trustworthiness give shape to a biblical understanding of the ways we must live alone or with others.

Theological Perspectives
on Living Alone

Again and again, theologians have made the same point about human life: We are communal beings. We are not created just for ourselves. A human being is destined to be in covenant with God. Part of the meaning of that covenant relationship with God is, for the human one, God's call to be in fellowship with others. The human creature is social through and through. Karl Barth is one theologian for whom communal destiny was the essential mode of being human. "Humanity, the characteristic and essential mode of man's being, is in its root fellow-humanity. Humanity which is not fellow-humanity is inhumanity."[10] We cannot be human without relating to others. And our relationship with God the Creator cannot be understood apart from our being with others.

More recently, John R. Sachs has made this same point in *The Christian View of Humanity*. We are most fully human in our relationship with others. "The paradox of human being as interpersonal is that what we truly need to live and to become self-actualized is something which I must receive as a freely bestowed gift from others. . . . We are dependent on each other!"[11] God's intention for humanity cannot be fulfilled without being with others in community. "Thus, the final good of each and every individual human person must be seen as the mutual interrelationship of persons in a community which includes all persons, in which each cares for the others and for the nonpersonal creatures placed in their care."[12] Persons who are alone and isolated are not likely to develop their gifts or attain their destiny.

A human community of both male and female most adequately images God as personal and relational. The mystery of the sexually other human is a symbol of the absolute mystery of God's otherness. We find both wholeness and fulfillment as we participate in the mystery of otherness. In that sense we can say that wholeness comes through the union of a man and a woman. Ordinarily, that union of different gendered persons is achieved through living with another in marriage. Marriage may be the ultimate form of relationship because it holds the greatest promise and possibility for finding wholeness. All aspects of our humanity can find full expression in the marriage relationship and so, by default, other relationships appear to be poor or inadequate substitutes.

While it is true that all aspects of our humanity can find full expression in the marriage relationship, it does not guarantee the experience of wholeness. Nor is marriage the only relationship through which human wholeness is possible. At various times in history and in a variety of places and for a variety of reasons, other forms of relationships have been greatly valued and those who embraced them held in high esteem. Think of monks, nuns, martyrs, poet-philosophers, protectors of the earth, and people of valor or perseverance. Each role has had its time of glory.

Once it is acknowledged that marriage itself does not guarantee a life-in-relationship-to-others that honors God's covenant with us, it is possible to see that other human relationships may provide both necessary and alternative ways of being whole. To be human is to be in relationship with others. To be human is to carry the image of God and God's ways with us into those relationships with others. God's way in us begins with our recognition of otherness and then the embrace of that otherness. God's gracious action and intention has the power to transform the human tendency to seek sameness. It is the courage to embrace the mystery of the other that enables us to discover our deepest self.

To be a Christian is to know that the human other is not perfect. Every relationship involves people who are in need of God's redemptive love, forgiveness, and empowerment. Because of that need, no relationship is without cost or free from the possibility of pain, betrayal, disappointment, or regret. Because of God's willingness to forgive and heal, we are enabled to go on with ourselves and with others to make and keep human life whole. Whether we are living with others in marriage or a family, living alone or with others as a single person, living in a religious community or a commune or a nursing home, it is both possible and necessary to discover ways of being in relationship with others through which to realize our communal destiny as humankind.

The Mystery of Otherness

Common wisdom, across time and cultures, would suggest that human completeness is found in the relationship between a male and a female. In that sense, the relationship of woman and man is paradigmatic of all relationships. Because woman is not man, nor man woman, we come to each other as "other." For all that men and women share in common as humankind, it is this "otherness," more than any common dimension of our humanity, that reflects our relationship to God, the one who is Wholly Other. Otherness is most profoundly symbolized by male and female, but it is not limited to gender differences. Whoever is "not me" is the other. It is in relating to others as distinctly "other" that traditional virtues like acceptance, reconciliation, fidelity, forbearance, and forgiveness make sense. To the extent that we are to emulate God's ways with us, these attributes become the marks of human wholeness and sustainable relationships.

Sexual intercourse between a woman and a man has been understood to be the ultimate form of relationship through which we discover wholeness. It is an experience of mutual giving that at the same time recognizes the uniqueness of each "other." Conception and birth are also relational events that recognize uniqueness as well. Every newborn infant is a unique personality beyond human reckoning. The relationship between a mother and her newborn child begins with the mother's awareness of the "otherness" of this new life. The newborn must establish and develop a relationship with mother, a being unknown until now, that eventually becomes an "other" to the child as well. If that is so, what can be said to those who live alone? Even when sexual intercourse was once a regular part of one's life or still might be an occasional dimension of living, we need to ask whether people who live alone have to settle for life without its basic and most characteristic relationship.

If we believe that we have been created *from* relationship *for* relationship, does the one who lives alone become something less than whole? This is the question that continues to haunt many who live alone, especially those who have always been single. Even if a single person is able to resolve the dilemma of sexual intimacy in a satisfactory and responsible way, it does not settle the fundamental, existential question: Can one live alone, be whole, and embody the intent of God for humanity? One might be good, admired, successful, attractive, faithful, intelligent, even heroic, but there always seems to be an essential ingredient missing. Even when it is understood that all relationships may become need-based, superficial, economic, episodic, manipulative, demeaning, or stifling, still those who live alone are often pitied. In order to respond more constructively to those who live alone, we need to continue to explore further God's intent for human life.

Living Alone and the
Friendship of God

What is finally distinctive about Christian anthropology is not the communal-autonomy paradox, essential as that is, but the declaration that the ultimate aim of human life is to be in relation with God. We are destined to be in covenant with God, and that relationship gives shape to our quest for understanding human relationships and human patterns of living. While God is wholly other, God is also near to us as friend. Theologian Sally McFague, in her book *Models of God: Theology for an Ecological Nuclear Age,* has introduced the image of friend as an alternative to thinking primarily of God's otherness.[13] She considers three images for God that relate to the traditional trinitarian formula while at the same time imagining God's ways of being with us in the present time. The image of God as friend provides a positive response to the question about living alone and being whole.

McFague proposes that images of God as mother, lover, and friend add an interactive character to traditional language about God as Father, Son, and Holy Spirit. It is McFague's contention that in each image, as in the whole, God's transcendence and immanence are both revealed. "In our understanding of the work of God in relation to the world, it is all of one piece: The creator says that it is good that you exist; the savior, that you are valuable beyond all imagining; the sustainer, that we shall all eat together, even the outsider."[14] Each of McFague's suggestions for perceiving God is worthy of attention, but it is the image of God as friend that seems to be a potentially rich resource for those who live alone.

The image of God as friend is not intended by McFague to promote equality with God or reinforce a desire for superficial chumminess. No image of God is adequate that does not promise to respect God's otherness. There are, however, numerous passages of scripture that present Jesus as friend in markedly egalitarian relationships. Even when Jesus identifies himself as Messiah, he does not, to use a common expression, lord it over others. His teaching does not coerce or manipulate in ways that we would recognize as the ploys of the powerful over the less than powerful. It is the mystery and the glory of the incarnation that God chooses to live as friend among those who are, in fact, God's creation.

Friendship is both a necessary and a complex dimension of human life. McFague is aware of our ambivalence toward friendship itself and especially the possibility of friendship with God. And yet, at its best, friendship is the most free of all human relationships. As McFague suggests, the basis of friendship is freedom. There are demands in all other relationships characterized by duty, utility, or desire. This recognition that friendship protects the freedom of the other undercuts the fear that God as friend would, in any way, be diminished or be less than the Other.

The image of God as friend provides a theological answer to our question: Can I live alone and be whole? One cannot find wholeness apart from being in relationship to others. To be persons-in-relation is the fundamental tenet of Christian anthropology. The gender of the persons with whom we may be in relationship and the specific nature of that relationship are more ambiguous. What is universally essential is that human life is inescapably communal. What is a matter of conviction is that God comes to each one as friend and, in accepting that gracious offer from God, no one need feel that she or he is all alone.

Summary

It is both a challenge and an opportunity to live alone as a human creature born for community. The freedom for both solitude and friendship is a distinct opportunity for those who live alone. The challenge is to actualize that opportunity in a balanced way that fulfills both sides of the autonomy/community paradox. To live for others as we were created to live, even as we live by ourselves; to be in touch with others by way of God's ways with us; to know a peace that does not ignore the pain of being alone; and to celebrate living alone as a calling that enables one to be among God's other children in a unique way are both goals and fulfillments.

When we accept living alone as one way of being with others for the common good, we are more likely to learn to live interdependently. Each person's gift is unique. The freedom to accept living alone as a calling is enhanced when we remember that others, whose gifts are different, are also created, redeemed, and gifted by God. In the world in which we live, the truly adventuresome and courageous are those who know their calling and set out to fulfill it.

2
LIVING ALONE AFTER LIVING WITH SOMEONE

LOSING A spouse is an emotionally painful experience that permanently changes many things. The loss of a spouse leaves a void both within the self and outside the self. Sometimes the self-understanding of the survivor is changed significantly. When death occurs in a family, the system changes as well. Some of the changes involve seemingly trivial activities once done by the deceased spouse, like shoveling snow, opening jars, or cooking the meals. Some people and some families respond constructively to those changes; others do not. Nonetheless, how we respond to the loss of a spouse or a significant partner shapes the remainder of our lives. *This book is about one consequence of the loss of a spouse: living alone.* Each of the following statements reflects something of the impact of the loss of a spouse on the surviving partner or the family as a whole.

—It was weeks before I stopped reaching for two of everything when I set the table. After a year of living alone, I still always make more coffee than I can drink.

—In the first months, I forgot to do the laundry because the laundry basket never overflowed.

—The first bank statement I had to reconcile made me outrageously sad and angry because it represented what I would have to do on my own from then on.

—I did not believe I could ever walk into church alone, and I knew I could not sing Harvey's favorite hymns without sobbing.

—My father always carved the turkey at Thanksgiving. Because no one wanted to take his place, we had ham instead.

—The care of my mother had been the center of my life for twenty years. Now that she has died, I must decide what to do with my life as a single person living alone. It is hard to start growing up when one is already forty.

Each response to loss is unique. It is determined by the nature of the relationship, the person of the griever, how the loss occurs, and the context in which the loss occurs. Those who have been prepared for mourning through other loss experiences will be able to recognize emotions and behavior that do not always seem to fall in the normal category. Learning to live alone after living with someone in marriage or in some other committed arrangement is a journey that begins in grief. Even when we may not be surprised by the loss itself, we are frequently unaware of how much and in what ways our life will change. Usually, though difficult to believe at first, the departure of a spouse, parent, or significant other is also the occasion for new freedom and more responsibility. Initially, however, the primary reality is loss.

We have used the category of loss in order to include ways other than death by which a relationship ends. Most commonly, the way we have in mind is a marriage that comes to an end when one spouse dies. The relationship may not be marriage, however, and the end may be divorce or leaving a love affair. The result, however the loss occurs, is the same: living alone. Because the capacity to mourn the loss is necessary in order to enter a new future, we begin this discussion on living alone after living with someone with a consideration of the dynamics of grief and grieving.

The term *living alone* emphasizes the distinction between living alone, ordinarily as a single person, and living with others, ordinarily—but not always—in marriage. It is possible to be a single parent but not live alone, in the sense in which we are using the category, because there are still children at home. It is also possible to be a single person living with others. As indicated in the introduction, living alone has an objective and a subjective meaning. Objectively, it means that the space one calls home is occupied by only one person. The subjective experience of living alone means to be without someone who is consistently involved in the ordinary and extraordinary decisions of daily living.

When Living Alone
Begins in Grief

It is inevitable for most couples that one partner will die before the other. When the death of a spouse occurs after the children have left home, the surviving spouse will ordinarily live alone, at least for a time. In the cycle of a family's history, this loss has a double meaning: one for the surviving spouse and the other for the system as a whole. There are other circumstances that lead to the possibility of living alone, like divorce, launching the last child as a single parent, the death of an elderly parent one has cared for, or the end of a long-term living relationship of friends or lovers.

> For me, the poignancy of living alone lies in knowing what a meaningful relationship can be. I lived with a woman for three years in my early twenties. We both worked part-time, so we had lots of time to spend with each other and with our friends. I moved away to go to school but continued to commute by train on weekends to be with her. When I got my first job, the relationship ended but I was still tied to her. It took me several years to grieve my way out of living with Marlene.   (Keith)

We have included Keith's story near the beginning to expand our awareness of the various experiences of living with others for which we grieve. At the outset, however, our focus is on the common situation of the death of a spouse after the children have grown. This moment also signals a significant transition for a family—the beginning of the end of one generation of a family's history. The ability of the family as a system to cope with death in the parental dyad will be shaped by its general openness to change and grief.

The inauguration of life alone for those who have lived with someone will be significantly affected by the nature of the loss itself and how one responds to it. A particular grief response has been understood in terms of (a) the relationship to the lost person or object, (b) the age of the deceased, and (c) the personality and gender of the grieving persons. Recently, Ginny Sprang and John McNeil have suggested that "the mode of death is a significant but overlooked dimension in the determination of grief responses."[1] We introduce this variable in order to suggest that how or when a person dies also affects the way people begin to live alone.

The Other Half of the Bed
is an Empty Sea

The death of a spouse is a traumatic disruption of life. If the marital bond has been positive, the grief is frequently overwhelming even when the death is expected. The full awareness of the scope of the loss does not usually begin for the surviving spouse until family and friends who gathered for the funeral have left. The experience of loneliness mutes the colors of the landscape for those who are alone after being with others. *The sudden quiet and growing sense of emptiness form the first context in which a newly widowed spouse begins to experience the reality of living alone.* The initial response is more like personal emptiness or a void in the family system.

> I never expected Liz to die first. She had to give up so much to take care of me when my eyesight began to fail. I hoped I would be first so she could have some time without my being a burden. Even after the doctor said her cancer was inoperable, I thought I would go first. We had been inseparable companions since I retired ten years ago. I know that Liz is dead but I still talk to her every night. I don't tell my friends or family what I do because they would worry that I have lost my senses. I tell her that I will be with her soon. In the meantime, Liz is a daily presence in my life. I still turn back the blankets on her side when I go to bed. When I wake up in the night, her half of the bed is like a vast empty sea. After fifty-one years of marriage, I do not know how to sleep alone.   (Robert)

For people like Robert, sleeping alone after having shared a bed with the same person for fifty-one years is the hardest adjustment. Others will say that eating alone is when the real loneliness sets in. Still others say they miss the simple exchange of ideas or comments about something they had read or seen on television. For others, they will miss having someone to come home to, pay the bills, light the water heater pilot light, or service the car. Others are aware, in a new and intense way, how many families there are at church or other public settings. It is not always possible to anticipate what will evoke the strongest reaction. We do not always know what we value the most until it is gone.

When a Long Relationship Ends

When a spouse dies after many years of marriage, there are two aspects of the initial response that influence the beginning of life alone. First, the adjustment to a different style of living is less dramatic for elderly survivors who have already altered their activities. Even so, the tasks of daily living may be more problematic because of a decline of strength, mobility, or finances for the surviving spouse. If death is understood as a natural process at the end of life, the trauma is lessened.

Second, for people who have lived together for a long time, there is a sense in which the surviving spouse does not live alone. Robert talks to Liz every day even though it would appear that he had accepted the reality of her physical death. Because many widows and widowers regard the dead spouse as a living presence, they do not always acknowledge that they live alone. Daily conversations with a deceased spouse can lead to contradictory action; the assurance of their presence may empower some newly widowed to be more open to new possibilities in life *or* it may occasion retreat into an increasingly more reclusive way of living, waiting for a reunion in the afterlife.

Third, unless some changes have been made as parents grow older and become less independent, the family may have some adjustments to make when an elderly parent dies. If the surviving parent cannot live alone, children and grandchildren may need to sacrifice some freedom. Even if the surviving elderly parent is capable of independent living, the family will have decisions to make that maintain a balance between providing needed assistance and honoring autonomy, as the following story illustrates. It is crucial that families anticipate the need to change when one grandparent dies.

> Both of my grandmothers were widowed near the ends of their lives. On both occasions, my family struggled with providing support. We were fortunate that both women were in good health and able to live independently. Requests from them for assistance with physical needs like shopping, banking, home maintenance, transportation, and the like were welcome and even encouraged. They did not want to be a burden. My father was distressed when they would pay someone to do what he could have done. However, it was the emotional needs of widowhood that created the most stress, in part because emotions themselves were always suspect in my family. Once the immediate grief and early mourning period was passed, my family far preferred that my grandmothers seek out new friends rather than seek emotional support from the family. It took years to strike a balance that met the needs of my grandmothers for support and my family's need for freedom. (Lydia)

Midlife Loss

The end of a relationship in midlife is a terrible thing even when it is expected. It evokes rage at the unfairness of life. *When a spouse dies suddenly in the middle of life, people live alone in the midst of the debris of broken dreams and shattered assumptions about life and one's place in the world.* After struggling to raise children, establish a career, and provide for the well-being of a family with the expectation of more leisure time in the later years, the person widowed in midlife feels cheated. It often takes longer for the surviving spouse in such situations to come to terms with living alone because they continue to postpone facing the reality of the loss. Moreover, if the death is the result of violent action or a stigmatized cause or after a very brief second marriage, the process of learning to live alone may be impeded by the stress created by the trauma of the death.

In a previous volume in this series, *Promising Again,* the time when children are being launched was described as an ordinary crisis for the couple. They need to make new promises to each other in ways that acknowledge the changes that have occurred in each partner and in the marital bond itself. The emptiness that parental couples ordinarily experience when the children are launched is magnified for a parent who lives alone. For those who live alone after the children leave home, it is a time to make promises to oneself. The freedom to discover hidden gifts covered over by parenting responsibilities is also the positive experience of single parents who live alone after the children leave. For many, it is like starting a whole new life.

When a Conflicted Relationship Ends

If the relationship that ends has been conflicted or ambivalent, a mixture of guilt and relief may immobilize a person's ability to mourn. The negative side of ambivalent feelings produce so much guilt that a person avoids all feelings. If the spouse of such a relationship dies, we are often impeded in expressing negative, as well as positive, feelings because we are not to "speak ill of the dead." *When it is difficult or impossible to grieve because of ambivalence about the relationship, people are stuck in a limited present without a past or a future.* One way to break the impasse is to make the private, internal "war inside" external. The process of expressing both positive and negative feelings unlocks the ambivalence and makes a new perspective possible.

> My husband had been an alcoholic for most of our married life. He had never been mean or violent. He seldom got drunk at home. He would just go away for days and we would not know where he was. I made up stories to tell the children about where he was, but I think they always knew. When he drank, he gambled. And when he lost, as he often did, he was verbally abusive to me. As a result we always struggled financially. About two years before he died, he stopped drinking. During that time he was the most wonderful husband I could have ever had. We talked together. We walked in the park. If only it had been that kind of marriage all the time. Even though the last years were good, I was relieved when he died. I did not want him to control the end of my life with sickness as he had controlled most of our marriage with alcohol.   (Violet)

People like Violet who survive conflicted marriages are often less overwhelmed by grief and more capable of immediate social participation. A study by Colin Murray Parkes and Robert S. Weiss, however, showed that the resolution of grieving in conflict-laden marriages is often not good. They offer the following reasons why: "It seems to us that the most obvious inference is that a report of a conflict-laden marriage can be taken as an indication of a relationship marked by ambivalence. Marital conflict had produced anger and, perhaps, desire for escape, but coexisting with these feelings were continued attachment to the other and even, perhaps, affection. Anger interfered with grieving, and only with the passage of time did a persisting need for the lost spouse emerge in the form of sadness, anxiety, and yearning."[2] Because the complexity of the grieving comes later, it often interferes with the process of adjusting to living alone.

Violet's initial response to her husband's death is common in marriages where ambivalence is present. Although Violet expresses relief at her husband's death, she was probably sad that he died just when their relationship had improved and angry that she had wasted so many years waiting for him to stop drinking. Ambivalence complicates the grieving process. The expression of grief seems hypocritical even though there was some attachment. Indeed, as Parkes and Weiss suggest, "ambivalent attachments can be harder to dissolve than unambivalent attachments. . . . It is difficult to mourn wholeheartedly when there was anger toward the dead as well as attachment, and difficult to understand one's own feelings when they are so mixed."[3] This ambivalence takes many forms in grief. If the so-called victim is the one who dies and the abusing spouse is the one who survives, the survivor may glorify the deceased spouse as if he or she was a saint in order to rectify the wrong of the past. It is common in conflicted marriages that death does not silence the critical voice of the deceased spouse. Violet's internal community probably included abuse from her husband long after he died. For spouses who survive a conflicted marriage, their capacity to function autonomously is often impeded by old voices declaring that whatever they do, it will turn out badly.

Living Alone after Divorce

The end of a marriage through divorce is often prolonged, and therefore discovering the pain of living alone after living with someone is more gradual. Sometimes the relief that a painful, troubled marriage has finally ended is so great that no sadness is allowed. On the other hand, someone who is left and did not want the marriage to end may continue to nurse hurt and anger in ways that make it hard to resume ordinary living. People who have been wounded by a divorce may try to punish the former partner by continuing to be miserable.

> After thirty-seven years of marriage, my ex-husband traded me in for a younger model. Everyone was surprised but me. We had not slept in the same bedroom for twenty years. Even so, I was angry and hurt and humiliated. My private sorrow has become public shame. As a result, I have not left the house for six months. Our sons tell me he did not get a very good deal on the trade. It serves him right. I feel more and more isolated from them because I cannot tell the truth about their father and our marriage. (Nora)

When a divorce occurs while the children are still young, the grief for that loss may not emerge until the last child leaves home. The process of launching the last child from a single parent family is emotionally complex even when there are no other complications. The silence is a source of both relief and terror. It is both sobering and comforting when the absence of adolescent energy makes it easier to order one's life at a pace for the middle years—sobering because the desire for a slower pace is a sign of aging and death, comforting because we do not have to keep trying to run faster than we can. Raising children as a single parent is hard work. Many women who are single parents describe their years with growing children as a time when they barely kept their heads above water. When the children leave, they take with them a weight of caretaking responsibilities. When the children are gone, there is freedom to breathe.

> Raising two daughters by myself without much financial help from their father has demanded all of my energy. I had my nose to the grindstone both at work and at home. I am proud of how we all turned out. My daughters are doing well and we have a great relationship. Most of all, I am delighted with the prospect of only having to care for myself. On the weekends, I eat when I am hungry and sleep when I want. I know my present euphoria about freedom cannot last forever. For the moment, however, I love doing what I want to do.   (Charlene)

Whatever the reasons for losing a spouse, living alone after living with someone begins in grief. The way a spouse dies or a marriage ends in divorce will affect the process of grieving itself and in turn affect one's beginning to live alone. For instance, survivors of a suicidal death have not only the usual pain of bereavement but also grief that is disenfranchised because the death was caused by unacceptable social behavior. "Shame, guilt, and self-denigration may be present as an integral part of the grief experience following several modes of death, but one could easily surmise that these feelings would be much more intense if the death were stigmatized."[4] As a result, the bereaved may be forced to grieve in solitary silence. And the loneliness of learning to live alone is exaggerated by isolation.

How the Family Changes as a Whole

The larger family unit must deal with some of the same things that the surviving spouse must face. Even when the death of an elderly parent is viewed as an integral part of the family life cycle, it is not without its stresses. Adult sons and daughters have dependencies on parents that often are not recognized until the parent dies. If a parent's death occurs in midlife, the family as a whole may participate in the denial in order to keep death away from ordinary family living. When the relationships between the deceased or divorced parent and other family members are conflicted or ambivalent, it is difficult to integrate that loss into the web of family life. As a result, family members may unwittingly participate in a response to loss that keeps the whole system stuck in the present without a future or a past.

> I have lived with my mother since my parents divorced fifteen years ago. For a while, my mother and I were on welfare. My two sisters and brother had already left home. When my son was born five years ago, I felt rage toward the baby I could not understand. Susan, my wife, insisted that I visit my father whom I had not seen in ten years. I met him a couple times with his fourth wife, but I stopped because it made me even more angry. I even tried therapy, but it did not help. When my father died last year, we read about his funeral in the paper. My sisters and brothers did not attend the funeral either.   (Jeffrey)

There are identifiable tasks of mourning that will enhance adaptation and further the life cycle development of all family members and the family as a whole. From what Jeffrey has told us about his family, we presume they are stuck in rage after fifteen years because the work of grieving has not been finished. Family therapists Froma Walsh and Monica McGoldrick have identified four tasks that need to be accomplished if the family as a whole is to move beyond any significant loss in the system.[5] We have modified their language slightly to take into account the reality that grief from divorce may be frequently as intense and often more complex than the death of a parent or spouse. We have added a fifth category that takes into account that the belief system of the whole family must be revised to take into account the loss that occurred.

1. *A shared acknowledgment of the reality of the loss.* The inability to share the loss blocks its resolution and leads to dysfunction in the family as a whole. Although the emotional responses to the loss will vary depending on the nature of the relationship between those who survive and the lost person, there needs to be clear and direct communication about the death or divorce and open communication about its consequences for every person in the family. The reluctance of adults to let children or grandchildren experience the loss may itself block the resolution of grief. It would appear that this communication has not taken place in Jeffrey's family—except around rage.

2. *Shared experience of the pain of grief.* Perhaps the most delicate task for families is to create an atmosphere of mutual understanding and acceptance so that people might express "complicated

and mixed feelings, including anger, disappointment, helplessness, relief, and guilt, which are present to some degree in most family relationships."[6] If family loyalty does not allow certain feelings to be expressed, or if the feelings are only considered in hushed tones, problematic behavior may occur. The need for shared experiences may be even more difficult to acknowledge if the one who died was the one in the family who historically made it possible for the family to function as a whole. It is possible that the persistence of rage in Jeffrey's life covers over yet another painful emotion: his mother's initial pain from the divorce.

3. *Reorganization of roles in the family system.* Every family is a network of assigned roles that has been developed to fulfill the family's needs and responsibilities. Roles need to be reassigned to compensate for what was lost. "The turmoil of disorganization during the transition period may lead families to try to hold onto old patterns that are no longer functional or to prematurely seek replacements in order to regain stability."[7] Ideally, this is a time for rethinking role assignments in the family in ways that allow for the designation of new roles. As long as Jeffrey was willing to continue in the role of caretaker, it will be uncontested by his siblings. It was, however, another way the family remained stuck.

> My mother was the family organizer and communicator. She died in an auto accident about a year ago. One month ago, my Dad told me that he will not make the arrangements for a family vacation at Lake Rubun next summer. Mom always did it before, but one of the kids has to do it, Dad said. So I organized a telephone conference with Dad, my brother, and sister to schedule and then reschedule a week at the traditional family lake cabin. I was very much aware all along that I was doing Mother's job. (Steve)

4. *Reinvestment in old rituals or family patterns even though they will not be the same.* If the role of the deceased person was to keep the family together or organize family gatherings, even when the roles are reassigned the family may undermine efforts toward family gatherings. Sometimes families stop telling stories altogether in order to avoid the pain of remembering the one who is gone. Members may insist that because Christmas will not be the same without Grandpa's gifts in paper bags, it should not be doing Christmas at all. In the previous story, Steve's willingness to organize the family gathering at Lake Rubun only gets the family to the cabin. The family needs to address what

makes the week special for everyone and then decide which of those traditions will be continued and how.

5. *Renewing the family's belief system.* Every loss, even those anticipated at the end of life, is a challenge to our ways of thinking about the limits of living. The death of a parent is an unmistakable sign of finitude for middle-aged daughters and sons. When meaning or purpose has been identified with the deceased parent, there is a vacuum in the family belief system. Sometimes, the death of the family member designated to be the moral agent is the occasion for family members to act out primary opposition to the moral position of the parent who has died. If the marriage has ended by divorce, the family may become stuck on anger and revenge in ways that corrode its moral or spiritual vitality. One would guess that Jeffrey's family has not replaced hurt and resentment with a spirit of forgiveness or graciousness for its members and the larger world as well.

These five categories address tasks that the family must respond to when a parent dies. The family also needs to modify its behavior toward the surviving parent. Some families become very protective and controlling of a surviving spouse and parent. As a result, the discovery of self that occurs in new ways when one must live alone is impeded by the well-meaning intentions of adult children to fill up all the emptiness. In a curious way, the motto for parents when their children are marrying needs to be the motto for children and grandchildren of a surviving parent: stay close and stay out. Living alone is a time of sadness. It is also the occasion for profound self-discovery. Families that are eager to resist further change may prevent that self-discovery by impeding the surviving parent's freedom.

Losing a Spouse: Making the Transition

Men and women respond differently to the loss of a spouse. Widowers "are at especially high risk of death and suicide in the first year of bereavement because of the initial sense of loss, disorientation, and loneliness, and because of the loss of a wife's caretaking functions."[8] Men are particularly vulnerable after the death of a spouse because they have been socialized to ignore their dependency needs. Moreover, the prohibition against publicly or even privately expressing emotions of sadness and grief contributes to male vulnerability when a spouse dies or a marriage ends in divorce.

For most women, the emotional components of the loss of a spouse are more readily expressed. Some widows have difficulty with the less emotional and more everyday tasks the husband did like paying bills, handling investments, fixing the plumbing, and moving. Elderly widows, whose husbands had handled all the financial responsibilities, may find themselves ill-prepared to live alone. Loss as a widow is often compounded by other dislocations, for example, "when the family home and social community are given up, or when financial problems or illness reduce independent functioning."[9]

The tasks are the same for women or men in responding to significant loss. First, gain emotional separation from the person who was lost. In order to *loosen the bonds* to the spouse, it is necessary to rehearse the memories of extraordinary and ordinary daily experiences. Remembering, as a part of grieving, aims at formulating a cherishable memory. Second, as a person gains more and more emotional separation from the deceased or divorced spouse, it is possible to turn toward the demands of daily living, self-support, and the support of the household. It is during this time that people will begin to make the physical and emotional *adjustment to the living alone phase*. Third, people who live alone begin to shift to new interests and activities and friends. We have identified this as the phase of *making a new life*. Grieving is a process of relearning our world that includes relearning our physical surroundings and our relationships with others and with God.

Loosening the Emotional Bonds

The most painful work of grieving is emotionally letting go of the person who has been lost. The aim of this process is to transform a lived experience in the present into a memory that is always past. The prerequisite for this grieving work is a recognition of the reality of the loss. In many instances, this realization comes slowly. It may be facilitated by the rituals that surround death. When the loss of a spouse happens through divorce, the final decree of a judge makes the end of a marriage real. Most mourners will say, however, that the full awareness of the loss, whether by death or divorce, happens over time.

> My grandmother said that the realization of my grandfather's death struck her most forcefully several months after his death. Late one night, she was awakened by a gentle tapping in her living room that intensified into a banging noise. When she

turned on the lights, she discovered that a mouse had been caught in a trap, but not killed, and was slamming the trap against her china closet in an effort to be free. She found herself crying on the back step, saying, "Bill, why did you leave me alone?" as she put the mouse in the trash. The next day she replaced the traps with poison. (Carter)

Telling stories about the lost person and remembering events from the past related to a bond that has physically ended are the most effective means for loosening the emotional claim of a marriage or long-term relationship. The intent of remembering is to build a memory of the past that can be honored in the present. It is important to have people who listen when we do the work of making a memory. Those who live alone need friends and family who will sit with them long enough to tell the stories needing to be told that will create an emotional scrapbook.

The second difficult work of grieving that loosens the emotional bonds is to dispose of clothes and other objects that remind one of the presence of the lost person. It is a process that must be done slowly. In the beginning, we need some reminder of the person to soften the grief. If, however, his clothes are in the closet just as they were when he left for work the day he died or her sewing room is cluttered and unchanged long after the death occurred, the grieving person may need some assistance in taking the next step toward loosening the bond. The step of loosening the bond is crucial for people who live alone because it creates the possibility of openness to the future. When the past has become a memory, the future is open for something new.

Adjusting to Living Alone

The second agenda for living alone after living with someone begins almost immediately after the loss. There are forms to fill out and financial decisions to make for which some spouses are not prepared. The major adjustment may be sleeping alone. Or it may be lighting the pilot on the water heater, changing a fuse, learning to pump gas, shopping for groceries, or cooking a meal. Learning how to do things one did not need to do because they were always done by the partner is a daunting challenge. So is finding ways to do things alone that are two person tasks, like hanging pictures, putting up the artificial Christmas tree, or getting into a dress that zips up the back. Some see it as a new adventure. Others are overwhelmed by the prospect of having to do things that they have not done before.

> Every holiday after Harold died was difficult. We always did the planning and decorating for Christmas together. The real shock came, however, when I got a notice from the IRS that I had not filed my tax forms. It had never occurred to me. I had even forgotten about our annual fight at tax time. When I had to figure out myself what to do about the taxes, I knew that Harold was really gone. (Jennifer)

For a time, it is understandable that every new thing persons must learn to do is a reminder of those who have died or gone away and therefore an occasion for grieving. Eventually, they must decide to learn how to do what they have never done before because nobody is there to do it for them. Or they may decide that what was done by a spouse will either not be done at all or done by others. Learning to live alone after living with someone will require shifts in self-perception that are beyond simply the doing of certain tasks. This will include facing inevitable dependencies in themselves not previously recognized. Men who are taught to be self-sufficient may find the discovery of dependency particularly difficult. Some marital relationships are designed around the covert rule that men should not be confronted with dependent behavior that is obvious to women in the relationship.

Shame is a common dimension of grieving. For men, part of the shame of grieving is the recognition of how much they depended on their partner who is gone. For women, the struggle may be the opposite because dependency has been presumed to be a feminine quality. As women adjust to living alone, they must decide whether it is possible to be more self-sufficient and whether they want to be a self-sufficient person. Sometimes widows have hidden their skills with auto repair, plumbing, or fixing machines so as not to be labeled one of "those self-sufficient women."

This decision has consequences for living alone. Men who decide they can never learn how to boil water will expect to marry as soon as possible in order to avoid learning to do things that do not fit their image of being a man. Women who would rather not learn how to do some things their husband used to do must change their self-perception or the way they live alone. Others, men or women, may regard this as a time to discover hidden gifts or at least begin a new life without all of the previous assumptions regarding gender.

Making a New Life

At some point, when the primary work of grieving has ended and preoccupation with adjusting to doing new things is no longer constant, people who live alone after living with someone must begin to take steps toward making a new life. The timing of this movement cannot be fixed. Friends and family who are eager for the time of grieving to be over are often too quick to insist that people resume their normal activities in the church or the community or in relation to family. Although these overtures may be well-intended, they are experienced by the mourning person as efforts to take the grief away.

The journey back from grief to ordinary social interaction is complicated by individual fears and social stigmas. Widows or widowers will often describe themselves like amputees. Their return to social activities is particularly terrifying for people whose marriage majored in togetherness. If they never went anywhere without their spouse before death, it is hard to imagine how they can appear alone now. For others, their return to former activities like the Friday pinochle group, square dancing, singing in the church choir, or the gourmet eating club is colored gray because of the lingering grief. Unfortunately, some people avoid previous relationships in order to avoid sadness.

For men, forming a new life is often cast in terms of dating or looking for a wife. "The number one reason a man starts to date and return to the coupled world is a need for companionship—someone just to talk with, to have dinner with, to fill the void brought about by the aloneness of being without a wife."[10] The chapter in which that quote appears is called "The Widower's Return to Life—to Love, Romance, and Sex." Implied in the title is an understanding that life is lived in relationships that are sexual. Most widowers hope that dating will ultimately lead to love and marriage.

> My husband and I had an island summer home in Massachusetts. This is my real home. I have lots of visitors to the island every summer. I drive on the beach with a four-wheel drive Jeep. I love to dig for clams and surf cast for bluefish. I give theme parties. I had a Greek party recently with appropriate decorations, food, and music. People look forward to my par-

ties and it provides me with weeks of activity. I have developed quite a reputation that I must keep up. I still get lonely, but when I do I make something happen.   (Wilma)

There are continuities between Wilma's world before her husband died and after. The island summer home is one continuity. It is quite possible, however, that her husband did not like parties. Her independence provides the freedom to relearn something that may have been dormant throughout her marriage. Finding our way after the death of a spouse is not about gaining new information but about learning how to be and act in the world differently in the light of our loss. Thomas Attig has described this process of relearning the world in this way:

> Relearning the world is a multifaceted transitional process. As we grieve, we appropriate new understandings of the world and ourselves within it. We also become different in the light of the loss as we assume a new orientation to the world. As we relearn, we adjust emotional and other psychological responses. We transform habits, motivations, and behaviors. We find new ways to meet biological needs. We reshape our interactions and connections with others. And we change understandings and interpretations and alter spiritual perspectives. Relearning is thus holistic.[11]

What Attig has described so well as "relearning the world" is not without risk. Those who prefer continuity to change are likely to minimize change. Because change inevitably involves risk, "relearning the world" in order to "make a new life" means that we must trust that which is unknown. Freedom to relearn our world when someone we love dies is, in this sense, an act of courage and faith. It will be easier if we believe that the future belongs to God. It will also be easier if we have the courage to be surprised, even by what we ourselves decide.

Living Alone after
Living with Someone

Learning to live alone after living with someone will, for a long time and perhaps always, be done in reference to the new responsibilities and freedom occasioned by the other's death or departure. The absence of another person will evoke changes in behavior and self-understanding: discovering dependencies, being aware of loneliness and the longing for sexual intimacy, sorting out family ties, and most of all, learning to live with grief.

Living with Grief

Grieving never ends. If we have loved someone fully and invested ourselves completely in a relationship with another, when that bond is severed the grieving never ends. The pains of grief will diminish. We will begin to make plans for the future. Sadness will not always catch us unexpectedly while we are at lunch with a friend, as it may at first. Even so, grief remains. For that reason, learning how to live alone includes living with grief. What makes that process complicated is that sometimes the loneliness of being alone triggers an awareness of the loss, which is the reason for living alone.

It is not always easy to distinguish between ordinary grief that inevitably lingers and chronic or stuck grief that must be removed. Beverley Raphael has defined chronic grief in a way that articulates the difference. "Months or years later the bereaved person still appears actively grief stricken, is still preoccupied with the lost person, visits the grave again and again daily or weekly; talks, thinks, feels nothing that doesn't relate to the death and the dead; cries at the slightest reminder; and is chronically angry, perhaps guilty."[12] Grief for the deceased is maintained by keeping clothes in place or a favorite chair clean or golf clubs polished and ready to use. It is not easy to tell whether those mementos are in place as a permanent memorial or because of the expectation of return.

Discovering Dependencies

When people live alone after living with someone, they are likely to discover dependencies they had not recognized. It is in the nature of relationships that they foster dependencies even when we are not aware of it. "Then when a spouse dies, we are suddenly without our usual source of support. Suddenly, we are forced to be self-sufficient all over again."[13] When the death of a spouse occurs later in life, the dependencies have accumulated over the years and have increased with the onset of aging. For some people, it is learning to be independent for the very first time.

Living alone after living with others is a double dilemma of dependency. On the one hand, people who have been used to having certain things done for them on a daily basis must now learn how to do them or hire help. For widows who have lived in a traditional marriage, the death of a spouse forces a new kind of independence. On the other hand, the death of a spouse reveals hidden dependencies on a spouse, particularly in men, that now become public. Things that were done for them without their asking must now be requested of others. Men, after the death of a spouse, must come to recognize their dependency in new ways.

Loneliness

After the grief is gone, loneliness remains. It is the inevitable condition of later life after a spouse dies. Other aspects of grief may subside as time goes on, but if no new relationship is formed to replace the one lost, loneliness continues. And it is not easily fixed. For "loneliness is the reaction to the *absence of the valued relationship* rather than to the *experience* of the loss."[14]

For many people who are widowed, the loneliness is exaggerated by being cut off from their previous company of friends who are still coupled. Most widowed people have to face a dramatic change in their social network. As a result, as Scott Sullender once observed, they are "both lonely *and* socially isolated after their spouse dies."[15] Unfortunately, this is something that increases rather than diminishes with time. It is, however, less problematic for men than for women.

The social stigma for widows or women divorcees is a reality that impedes their easy return. Everyone can tell horrible stories about such a person who was cut off from previous social networks or shunned by couples with whom she had been close before the death or divorce. As a result, widows often end up making their new life with other widows and further isolating themselves.

The dominant emotional dynamic of people who regularly live alone is loneliness. Although it is certainly present in the other circumstances of living alone, for those who have always lived alone loneliness and solitude are part of the permanent landscape. Living with silence is a major part of living alone. In order to be content with living alone, one must make friends with solitude. That adjustment will be easier for some people than for others; there are those for whom a lifetime of living alone is colored with a loneliness that will not go away. In each of the subsequent chapters, we will consider anxiety, loneliness, and solitude in relation to specific dimensions of living alone. For those who live alone after living with someone, however, the overwhelming dynamic is one of sadness and grief.

Desire for Sexual Intimacy

Sexual intimacy, usually a significant dimension of a marriage and often of a long-term relationship, will be a particular loss when the spouse or sexual partner is gone. Older survivors may be reluctant or unwilling to even imagine exposing their obviously aging bodies in acts of intimacy. Some, for whom sexual intimacy was seldom a good experience, may be relieved that the demands are gone. Most, however, will have to deal with the natural longings of their bodies and their spirits. Responding to these longings may take a variety of forms, from a series of sexually active relationships to disciplined abstinence. Some response, however, is unavoidable.

As it is with people who have always been single, those newly alone will have to explore and discover ways in which they can know sensual and sexual satisfaction. First of all, however, when the ache of missing being touched, held, and loved is most present and painful, it is important to acknowledge the desire for sexual intimacy without fear that such an admission will lead automatically to acting on it. Having to hide the longing only makes it worse. Losing a sexual partner does not mean we stop being sexual persons. We will return to this important theme in the next chapter.

Sorting Out
Immediate Family Bonds

This sorting out task is the other side of the family's response to loss. The surviving spouse will need to establish a pattern for interacting with children and grandchildren that nonetheless allows time to be alone. For elderly persons, some of whom outlive siblings and even their own children, the sadness after a spouse dies has the character of being bereft. Without children, the person who lives alone after marriage is often expected to return to the family of origin as the primary source of support. For the parent who lives alone, relationships with children are exceedingly important. The connections with grown children will be more complicated, however, after divorce. The following statements convey what parents need, hope for, and receive from their adult children and grandchildren.

—My two children offer no hindrance or difficulty to my living alone. I believe they are glad I am able to take care of myself—mentally, physically, and fairly well emotionally.

—I was divorced without children. I no longer have any family. While they lived, I wish my family had realized that living alone was not as easy for me as they thought.

—I have a son living out of the country. We stay in touch by fax. My other children are not so faithful. I see my only grandchildren every other weekend. They help me out a great deal.

—My children have not made it easier or harder to live alone after the divorce. I do sense their concern about the spatial inequities of their parents. Their visits to town are complex because their parents live only a few blocks apart.

—I have a daughter, son-in-law, and two grandchildren nearby. We are very close and that makes a big difference.

—We write more than call. I feel close to one child but I know that the other would come in emergencies. The only neglect I feel is when the interval between letters seems too long.

—I think if I were not living alone—if I had a husband—my children would assume that I was getting along just fine and I probably wouldn't hear from them as often as I do now. My children both keep in close touch and are very interested in what I am doing with my life.

When the family's impulse is to treat the surviving parent as fragile or needing constant attention, the parent may need to set clear limits in order have the experience of living alone. In cultures where the expectation is that parents do not live alone when they are old, living in a son or daughter's home may be a reassuring gift of love and an affirmation that they are still needed. It could also be another loss. When the grandparent is expected to help with parenting grandchildren, new boundaries may need to be established to honor the freedom of a surviving parent. Sometimes, the death of a spouse allows the surviving parent and grandparent to have relationships that were not possible while the other spouse lived. Hopefully, new patterns of interacting will continue and deepen bonds of affection while at the same time honoring freedom for both adult children and the surviving parent to discover new dimensions of themselves.

Summary

The experience of living alone after living with someone in marriage or another relationship of intimacy is expressed in many different ways. Grief is nonetheless a constant companion. In order to be content with living alone, one must also learn to live with loneliness and make friends with solitude. Learning to live alone takes time. For people who have always lived alone, there is an identifiable process that people go through that leads to acceptance. Understanding that process will also benefit those who live alone after living with someone.

3

ALWAYS LIVING ALONE

LIVING ALONE is increasingly common in our culture. A great many who live alone have previously lived with others in marriage or some other communal arrangement. Others have always lived alone. They are single people who left their familial home as young adults and immediately or eventually established themselves in a place of their own. Although some of these people may have decided to live alone from early adulthood or before, living alone is for some an unexpected or even unwelcome circumstance. Being a single person and having to live alone is particularly painful if it is not an individual's choice. Easy explanations will not remove the grief that is experienced when the cherished dream of marriage is unrealized. Instead of easy answers or solutions, we propose in this chapter to offer new perspectives on living alone, new ways of responding to the realities of living one's life alone, and new possibilities for hope and expectation.

> I always thought I would be married by now. At thirty-five I have become increasingly anxious because the hopes and dreams of marriage and family are less bright than they were ten years ago. Living alone was all right while I established myself in a career, developed a social life, acquired things of value, found out about myself, learned to live independently, and gained some emotional distance from my family of origin. I am very glad to have lived alone these years. But I didn't expect it to go on forever. Time is quickly slipping away. I feel more lonely, the quiet is more oppressive, and my family and friends make more comments about when I intend to settle down. I am settled but I would like to be married.   (Carol)

I have always been a free spirit, following the happenstances of my life with a sense of adventure. I am comfortable with living alone, although once in a while I worry about growing old alone. However, just the thought of adjusting to someone else's ways of doing things reinforces my continuing desire to live alone. It certainly is the lesser of two evils. Now I am sixty-three. I have enough people in my life to feel fulfilled. I have a sense that living alone has been right for me even though there have been times through the years (especially when all my friends had small children) when my self-confidence slipped away and I had to think and feel my way again to an acceptance of my life. (Lucinda)

These two stories convey an important truth: Living alone is experienced by different people in different ways. It is even different for the same person at different times in life. What was a necessary developmental strategy for Carol eventually lost its appeal. Lucinda had an easier time with her married friends after their children left home and everyone was childless. There are also personality factors that affect the response to living alone. Some would appear to be better suited for the experience than others. For some people, living alone is to be endured, for others it is occasionally satisfactory, for still others it is a desirable way of living. Some people appear to live all their days feeling incomplete, unfinished, as though they are missing a part of themselves. Others, however, seem comfortable with who and what they are. It is necessary to attend to these differences while at the same time identifying common themes in living alone.

I don't remember exactly when it happened, but my family and friends stopped asking when I would marry. About that same time, it also was clear to me that my mother was proud of me for my career, my education, and *who I had become* even though I had not married. I do remember the feeling of relief when I realized that my non-marital status was no longer a topic of conversation when the family gathered. (Virginia)

The ordinary struggles of living alone are further exaggerated by expectations from family and society. Virginia is fortunate. Her family finally stopped asking about marriage. Moreover, it was clear to Virginia that her mother accepted who she had become even though it did not include marriage. The questions confronting those who live alone come from without and from within. Despite the growing number of single households, people who live alone struggle against feeling incomplete because of expectations from society and from our families. While the focus of this chapter is on the experience of always living alone, people who live alone after being with others will find much of this discussion applicable for their life as well.

Expectations to Marry

It is hard for single people to cope with the complexities of life alone when they must frequently do battle with what the world seems to be telling them about their status. And if the expectations from society or family about being married are internalized as part of an individual's ideal, living alone seems like failure. It is empowering, therefore, to be able to claim for oneself that way of living. Neither passively capitulating to social or familial expectations nor choosing a way of life that challenges those expectations are life-enlarging options. They both point to the possibility that living alone for some people is a consequence of incomplete separation from one's home of origin. For that reason, being comfortable with living alone, despite the expectations, depends in part on leaving home successfully.

From Society

The expectation that people will marry and have children is universal in human societies. For some time, the adult who chose to remain single was regarded as failing in his or her duty to increase the tribe. The future of generations depended on having children, and marriage was eventually the context for having and raising children. The universal necessity for everyone to marry and procreate has diminished in our time because of population growth, but the social expectation to marry lingers. As a result, the social message remains the same for people who have always lived alone: Who they are and how they are living is inadequate. Social expectations are reflected in terms like "never married" that are used to describe "always living alone." It is not surprising, therefore, that some (but certainly not all) people who have "always lived alone" feel dissatisfied, angry, lost, or mildly or greatly depressed all or much of the time.

For those who believe that the well-being of a society depends on stable families, there is additional pressure to marry and stay married.

The primary message is that women and men should marry and stay married for the good of the children and the good of the society. The secondary message is this: We need to promote marriage in hopes of lowering crime, disease, and poverty rates. The assumption behind this secondary message is that men must be socialized or tamed by marriage in order to be good citizens. The male pattern of procreating without parenting, the assumption goes, not only creates hardship for women and children, it also does not initiate men into a pattern of adult male responsibility. According to Don Browning, "many ecologists believe that human evolution took a great step forward when biological fathers became invested in their children."[1] From this perspective, living single and alone does not contribute to a stable society.

While the population of single persons who live alone continues to increase, marriage remains a significant marker in the progression from dependency to adulthood. The authors of the book *Single in a Married World* make this observation: "One would think that this would be the ideal time for single people to live. Nevertheless, single people continue to feel alienated from the larger society, and those who enter therapy in the 1990s still feel acutely aware of their *differentness.*"[2] While we may not regard single persons as sick or assume they are immoral as we once did, they still seem less than the norm. People who live alone are regarded as incomplete. Because they have not met society's expectations about marriage, it is easy to regard them as second-class citizens or worse.

From Family

Cultural attitudes about being a single person are related to the role of the family in society. Some families worry about adult children who live alone. For other families, the absence of marriage and children brings shame to parents who feel that they have failed in their roles because their children cannot or do not marry. If it is assumed that the transition from the parental home into adulthood occurs through marriage, a family may resist other ways of moving toward adulthood rather than modify their embrace of a traditional pattern. Society sets the norms for what constitutes adulthood, but it is often the family that exercises the pressure to be married. Mothers have been known to be relentless in their determination to get a son or daughter married. It is not unnatural for parents to want their children to marry and have children, for their children's sake as well as for their own desire for grandchildren.

> My friends know that I live alone. Most of them know that I have always lived alone. I am always surprised, therefore, when people who know me well say to me about their own young adult child something like "we just hope and pray that one of these days she'll get married." They say it like they want their child to be rescued from a fate worse than death. I don't take it personally anymore, but I do wonder sometimes what they think about how I live.   (Rhonda)

It is not likely that Rhonda's friends are as insensitive as the story suggests. Even so, the total lack of comprehension on the part of a parent telling someone like Rhonda who lives alone about the "fate worse than death" that awaits an unmarried child is a hurtful thing. Most of all, the story illustrates the power of parental expectations that their children will marry. When the perspective of parents is that marriage is necessary for adulthood, adult daughters or sons are sometimes trapped between permanent childhood or rejecting their home of origin. It is not unusual that when people marry to fulfill the expectations of others, whether family, friends, or society, they may end up envious of people who live alone.

From within Oneself

There is, according to Judith Viorst, an enduring longing in every human to recapture in some way the experience of "oneness" or connectedness with which each of us begins life. Giving up this longing is one of the necessary losses in life, what we must give up to grow up.[3] Letting go of expectations is an ongoing human struggle. Expectations from society and from family about what it means to be an adult are often internalized. When that happens, it is difficult to separate our own dreams from the dreams of others. Most individuals, however, expect to marry as part of *their own* hopes for a fulfilling life. Letting go of those dreams is an experience of intrapersonal loss that we must mourn.[4]

> I never have and may never in the future absolutely decide to live alone always. There is *always* the possibility that I might live with another, not just out of necessity because I am weak, but by choice. I think I would be quite unhappy if I thought I had no choice in the matter.   (Donald)

The possibility of living with others makes living alone an act of freedom. Likewise, the capacity to live alone is necessary in order to live well with others. For Donald, freedom within himself either to live alone or to marry was crucial. That freedom is not possible for everyone. For some, the desire to marry may be motivated by the *fear of being alone*. If, for example, one of your most vivid memories of childhood is the time your parents left you almost entirely on your own while they attended to something else, the sense of fear and abandonment that you remember from that time may keep you perpetually uneasy in the quiet and solitariness of living alone. This same dread of abandonment may motivate others *to* live alone so as to avoid the possibility of abandonment. Being alone is experienced as a loss of self, a feeling that no one knows or cares about your life. As a result, the dread of abandonment becomes the motivation to marry or live with others in some way.

> Both my mother and grandmother were unhappy widows. After I left home, they each lived alone and complained about being alone. For me, becoming married was a carefully planned campaign. My motivation was not love first of all—it was my determination not to be unhappy like my mother and grandmother. I also felt a kind of urgency about it. If I didn't marry before thirty, I thought, it would never happen. I was fortunate to catch a medical student to whom I am still married. He does not know, however, that our marriage is the result of a calculated campaign. (Marlene)

> I don't know a lot of men who have always lived alone, but I know plenty who are trying to do it after divorce. Most of the time, I think I can handle it. My job keeps me busy, I work out four nights a week and help out at the church on weekends. When I do feel lonely, it's awful. I feel like a kid again. My parents both worked and I was an only child. I remember thinking that no one really knew where I was or what was happening to me. Driving from place to place, going to movies alone, or just being in my house, I sometimes feel the same way. Having a cellular phone does not help when nobody calls.

> (Christopher)

Early childhood experiences could also lead one to *live alone in order to avoid intimacy*. When relationships with parents or other nurturing persons is experienced as suffocating, people may choose to live alone in order to avoid intimacy. Facing the fear, you may come to realize that the experience of childhood and the experience of living alone as an adult are not the same thing, that anger at the parents who instilled the initial fear in you can be worked through, leaving you free to know yourself and trust yourself even when you are alone. The freedom to be comfortable living alone partly depends on the satisfactory resolution of negative childhood experiences that may push one either to seek or avoid intimacy as a way of circumventing the dread of abandonment.

Coming to Acceptance about Living Alone

No one's life turns out quite the way he or she expects. Everyone needs to make peace with the reality that perfection is not possible, nor can all our dreams be realized. Every circumstance of living carries a combination of pain and pleasure, satisfaction and frustration, fulfillment and disappointment. To name what one has and what one misses and to recognize those realities in others' lives is to begin a process of taking hold of one's life. People who have always lived alone describe that process of coming to some acceptance of their life in a variety of ways.

> The triggering event for me in struggling with the realization that I would probably always live alone was buying my first home. I always thought couples bought houses and homes are where we raise children. So did my real estate agent. I was the first single homeowner she had ever worked with. It was a major sea change for me and for my family. Going home was *not* to my parent's house but to my house. Relatives came to my *home* for holiday celebrations. (Connie)

In many instances, coming to terms with living alone will occur because other decisions have to be made. For Connie, it was buying her first home. For others, it may be ending a long relationship that had seemed to be moving toward marriage. This process of acceptance is enhanced by naming what is good and what is painful about living alone. Naming does not make the bad worse and nor will it make the good disappear. But it does help to look more realistically at those others whose lives we may otherwise see through rose-colored glasses. It also means deciding to make the best of a situation that is less than perfect.

It occurred to me quite suddenly one day that I regularly got depressed around 4:30 P.M. on Fridays. It was not just weariness from a long week of work but sadness tinged with melancholy. My assumption was that everyone else in the world was hurrying home to someone whom they loved and who loved them. I was the only one going home to an empty apartment. Once I was aware of that feeling, I began to see some other things as well. All the people who had people to go home to were not especially eager to get there. Being aware of that did not eradicate my 4:30 Friday feelings, but knowing that I could not feed my sadness with fantasy made the next step easier. I could take care of myself during that time, I could do whatever helped to get through that period . . . run errands, make plans with friends, listen to good music or read a good book, work out, buy myself flowers, visit someone who might be even lonelier than I was.   (Freda)

Freda's determination not to be stuck in a weekly cycle of sadness is only one illustration of a variety of decisions people who always live alone need to make in the process of coming to terms with their life. There is no set sequence to that process. There are, however, at least four resolutions to be made about living alone on the journey toward acceptance. Although we have cast these resolutions in declarative form, coming to terms with them occurs retrospectively in a process happening over time: (1) I am not likely to marry in the foreseeable future. (2) I am more than a respondent. (3) I am a whole person. (4) I can say no without being selfish.

I Am Not Likely to Marry in the Foreseeable Future

Marriage is *the* prior question for most people who always live alone. It is seldom settled in an absolute way. Marriage remains a possibility in the future, as it did for Donald in an earlier story, but the present reality of not being married is accepted. Most young adults who are not married will describe their status with phrases like "I am not married yet." Reaching the age of thirty-five was a startling reminder to Carol, in the story at the beginning of this chapter, that she may not be able to say "I am not married yet" forever. Sooner or later, people who live alone admit they are not likely to marry.

In 1956, when I was in the fifth grade, I decided that I did not want to have a typically woman's job like teaching, nursing, or being a secretary. I didn't know what I wanted to do, but I knew what I did not want to do. One of my mother's favorite cousins who came to visit us often had never married. She was educated, had a great career, and I don't remember anyone ever feeling sorry for her because she wasn't married. In fact, she was greatly admired in the family. Throughout my working career, even in part-time college jobs, I met women who lived alone. They were happy, energetic, fulfilled women. Knowing them shaped my thinking about living alone. I don't remember ever saying "I am not married yet." Eventually, I had a fulfilling, enjoyable, and creative career. Marriage wasn't *on my mind*. It was somewhere in the *back of my mind*. If I didn't enjoy my work, perhaps I would have thought more actively about marriage.

(Virginia)

Virginia's story is important for several reasons. In retrospect, she is aware that many factors have shaped her way of living. The acceptance of the reality that one is not likely to marry does not automatically lead to living alone. People who are not married may choose to live with someone for a number of reasons. Today, however, more and more people who are not married are socially and economically free to live alone.

I Am More Than a Respondent

Human beings are responding creatures. Our ability to respond creates relationships and sustains bonds of affection. If, however, we are defined only by being a respondent, we wait for life to come to us. And when it doesn't, we are inclined to permanently perceive ourselves as victims. To stay a victim of anything is to deny the image of God in oneself and demean the purpose for which each of us is created and redeemed. To allow life to simply happen to us is, in some sense, to consent to being a victim of fate instead of a participant in the life God intends for each of us.

In recent decades there have been scores of books written and hours of advice dispensed regarding the positive values of taking charge of one's life. Books similar to Bernard Siegel's *Love, Medicine and Miracles*[5] offer useful strategies for taking control of one's life under a variety of stressful conditions. Cancer patients are encouraged to visualize their bodies' war against the cells that would destroy them, abused people are supported in their refusal to stay victims, sexually harassed women are urged to stand up for their right not to be dealt with as an object or thing, teenagers are challenged to resist rather than succumb to peer pressure to do drugs or have sex. The following story illustrates how important it is to define oneself as someone who acts as well as responds.

> When I was about forty-five, I attended a weekend retreat in which the participants were asked to create an epitaph for their tombstones. I decided that my epitaph might read "She Responded" and for a while I felt pretty good about such a comment on my life. On further reflection, I realized that the epitaph suggested that I was always waiting for something to which I could respond (marriage was undoubtedly one of the "somethings" for which I was waiting). This awareness made me realize that I had a life, just one, and that I was more than a little responsible for what that life might be. Being about as adventuresome as Chicken Little, I did not rush out to climb Mt. Everest, move to a cabin in the woods, or make a reservation at Club Med (although any of those might be great choices for others), but I did stop waiting and started claiming my life for myself. It was about that time that I decided to start sending a mimeographed Christmas letter. I had read countless letters from couples about children and grandchildren and all that family life brought to daily life. I thought, well, people like me have a life too, so why not tell my friends about it? So I did.
>
> (Freda)

If we believe that we are only acted upon and seldom actors in our lives, we are provided with someone or something to blame for what we don't like about living alone or being single. To recognize that life consists of living with what we have and what we can make of it is to take responsibility for our life and to do what we can to make it good for ourselves and a gift for others. What Freda did to communicate with her friends and her wider community by letter at Christmas is wonderfully symbolic of the human need for agency. By narrating her story for wider telling, Freda also becomes an active agent in formulating a story that will become her gift.

I Am a Whole Person

The recognition that the person living alone is fully adult is essential for those who always live alone in order to come to accept its possibilities and limitations. Every individual already possesses, from birth, the fullness of being human. Children are not incomplete adults. Neither are those who are single and live alone. From birth, we are as fully human as we will ever become. People living alone have the same feelings, hopes, needs, and commitments as those who are married or otherwise living with others. If, however, marriage is understood to be the "royal road to adulthood," people who live alone struggle not to regard themselves as less than whole.

> For many years I would make up an excuse not to accept a last minute invitation for Friday or Saturday evenings, wanting others to think that I, of course, already had plans. I assumed that last minute invitations were prompted by charity or by the need to fill an empty chair at the dinner table at the last minute. I felt sorry for myself for not having a date and wounded because I had received a late invitation. I would say to myself that it was a matter of pride as I spent Saturday night wounded and alone. It was not until a friend of mine, whose late invitations I had turned down twice, convinced me that *she invited me to make her party better* that I was able to be glad for late invitations.
>
> (Martin)

Martin carried within himself self-doubt that may have had its beginnings in adolescence. Not to be asked and then, if asked, to doubt the reason for being asked are usually patterns of behavior that originate in the hurt and bewilderment of childhood. At one level, Martin's choice was simple: turning toward life or turning away from life. The possibility of wholeness for those who live alone requires reframing old hurts, taking risks, and making choices for one's own life. We may not always have a plan for a Saturday except to spend an evening home alone. That is enough, however, even though it may not be as good as spending the evening in the company of friends.

I Can Say No and Not Be Selfish

If someone lives alone, she or he is usually viewed by the rest of the world as someone with no responsibilities and lots of free time. People who live alone may not feel they have a good excuse to say no to any request for help. People who are married or live with others are less free because they appear to have more obligations. If an aging parent becomes ill, single sons or daughters who live alone are almost always expected to be the ones to set aside their life and their work to attend to the parent. Single people who live alone are the ones often asked to work overtime or be the designated driver because no one is waiting at home for them. While it is true that single people are often excluded socially in a "couples society," it is paradoxical that because more is expected of them in the work arena, they have even less time to develop the type of relationships they may want and that would certainly make them more socially acceptable.

Not infrequently, persons living alone feel guilty for spending time on themselves at the expense of getting a job done. Other times, however, the problem is quite the opposite: they only think of themselves. Those who live alone are particularly challenged to be good to themselves without losing sight of the gift of freedom for service, compassion, and hospitality to others. People who live alone are also expected to be more generous with their gifts because they are not putting children through college. There is an unfortunate assumption, often silently held, that those who live alone should be infinitely flexible and totally self-sacrificing. Facing a holiday alone may be difficult and working on a holiday may be an attractive alternative, but it should be an individual's choice and not an unspoken expectation.

> No one knows that I send money to an almost destitute elderly relative or that I worry alongside a sibling about the child who is embarked on a treacherous path. Likewise, people who expect that my life can be put on hold do not seem to realize that when I want to have a conversation, get advice, or play I usually have to schedule it some time in advance and arrange for it to happen.
> (Jerry)

It is unrealistic and sometimes even hurtful to presume that people who live alone "don't have any worries" so they are free to respond quite spontaneously to new challenges at work or in the neighborhood. Jerry's story reminds us that people who live alone may have significant but secret commitments and obligations to others. What is often overlooked about the experience of living alone is that every desired personal interaction must be initiated and scheduled or arranged. People who live with others might have equally or even more complex schedules, but they are not alone if the scheduling is not done.

> What I hate most about living alone is that I have no one to challenge my choices on a regular basis. I can live life for myself, on my own terms, to a greater extent than those who live

with others. No matter how worthy I may be in my own eyes, I shop for one, cook for one, clean up after one, and choose for one when it comes to deciding where and how to spend money, time, and energy. Or I may choose to spend all my time serving or helping others. I have no one to help avoid the extremes—selfish, self-centered existence or total neglect of the self in order to care for others. (Matthew)

The dilemma Matthew has described is a conundrum for everyone. How do we avoid the extremes of selfishness or self-sacrifice when there is no one to regularly challenge our actions? For the Christian person, the question is the same. How do we live as Christ's disciples, those called and gifted for participation in God's redemption and re-creation of the world and nurture the self that God created for that participation? These are, of course, questions for everyone, but for the one who lives alone they may have a peculiar urgency. And this is particularly difficult for women who were socialized to believe that self-sacrifice is the norm for them. People who live alone after being married often have children who will challenge the choices they make. Coming to terms with living alone means deciding that it is possible to say no without being selfish. People who live alone and people who live with others face the same dilemma: They need to find a balance between self-sacrifice and self-care.

While all people must finally claim a lifestyle for themselves, those who live in daily relationship with others will have the benefit and burden of others' affirmation or rejection of their claims. Living alone makes one especially vulnerable to second-guessing the motivation for the choices one makes. In the light of this awareness, active participation in a community of faith (or some voluntary community of unconditional regard) is essential in order to provide a context for ongoing dialogue about the shape and intent of Christian life.

The Dilemmas of Living Alone

Understanding it as gift does not resolve all of the tensions or dilemmas that occur to those who live alone. Moreover, what constitutes a dilemma is determined by past experiences and by expectations of future living. Because each person will settle them differently, we offer the following as suggestions toward more constructive ways of living alone.

Holidays

Most holidays have developed as family celebrations. Even though some family holiday patterns of being together change over the years because people and circumstances change, the longing to be "home for the holidays" remains. People who are unhappy living alone are doubly unhappy at holidays because everything reminds them of what they are missing. Nostalgia cancels negative memories or painful disappointments of the past. During holidays, perhaps more than any other time, those who live alone are tempted to feel like victims of forces beyond their control. It usually takes special planning to avoid holiday negativities. Whatever one plans at holiday time, as a person living alone one must factor in the expectations of family, as the following stories illustrate.

> Because of my job, I was not able to be with my family for Christmas or Easter for twenty years. For the last ten years, a group of people, some who live alone, some couples, some families with children, gathered to celebrate the holidays together. Last year, I was with my family. I was glad to be there but I really missed the people, the customs, the rituals of my holiday group. How do I tell my parents and siblings that I would rather be elsewhere at the holidays?   (Mark)

> Ever since I moved geographically away from my family, I have spent Christmas with them. Most of the time, I am bored when I am with my family. They insist on treating me as a child and I am accustomed to caring for myself. Two years ago at Christmas, I decided to go to Italy with some friends. I had a wonderful time, but my family felt rejected because I had chosen not to spend Christmas with them.   (Elsa)

Those who have always lived alone are often expected to return to the homes of their origin since they never married and do not have a family of their own. The dilemma facing those who live alone is whether to fulfill the expectations of family, setting aside a network of friends like Mark had, or return to the family patterns of one's origin, determined to remain the person one has become. Family plans for holidays may be further complicated by geographic distance, elderly parents living with one child or in a residential facility or nursing home, and demands of work. Any of these can make even the best-loved and cherished experiences of earlier holidays less and less likely to repeat. Families, including their members who live alone, need to rework holiday expectations so they fit present circumstances.

Children

It is not possible for everyone, even if they marry, to fulfill the deep yearning to be a parent, to live with and nurture children. For some, this longing may be deeper than the desire to be married or to live with other adults. There is no shame in the wish to have a child; it is a dimension of our created destiny to be in community and exercise our created capacity to conceive and bear children. The new possibility—adopting children as a single person—is a reality that may make the loss of children even harder to bear for those for whom it was not such an option. The dilemma is that adoption, like having a child for married people, must be considered openly and realistically because children take time, energy, financial resources, and sacrifice.

Having children is not the only way to participate in children's lives. All the jokes about old maid aunts and bachelor uncles cannot tarnish the joy that comes from having the time, the money, or the interests to share with nieces and nephews. It is a gift for children as well, to have uncles, aunts, and other special adults who are free to relate to children as caring adults without the responsibilities and limitations of parenting. Sometimes, the pain of not having children of one's own is preserved, held close, always available to evoke tears, great sadness, or acute pain. When that happens, it can become a wall that allows no other child in and thereby intensifies the loss. Even if the pain is acknowledged, maybe more than a few times in one's life, it should not diminish the freedom to spend oneself and one's love on other people's children. From the perspective of children, every child benefits from having someone like uncle Alex.

> Because I come from a large extended family, I have always had lots of children in my life even though they were not my own. My nieces and nephews have a special place in my life. Each one has been on at least one trip with me. I have also been a gift to them. To me, they have always been persons first, not children, perhaps because they were not *my* children. I allow them to do things their parents (my siblings) would not allow. On at least two occasions, I was the one that encour-

aged my nieces to leave home even though it irritated my sister a little.   (Alex)

Acknowledging what is missing, be it a deceased spouse, an estranged companion, or the children one never had, is a step toward both realism and some degree of resolution of the loss that is a prelude to greater personal fulfillment. The questions of career, the need for space and time for oneself, an awareness of a tendency to make the "other" what you want that one to be instead of nurturing the uniqueness of that individual, the home and environs in which a child would be raised—such issues need careful consideration before anyone fulfills their own need to have a child. Like getting married, finding a housemate, deciding to travel with a friend or a group of strangers, or changing jobs, the decision to adopt a child, take foster children, or even get involved with particular children in a tutorial program or a hospital visitation program is a decision to become vulnerable and to trust in God's guidance as one seeks to live for others and care for one's self.

Sexuality and Sensuality

As we have discussed earlier, human beings are sexual beings. We do not easily forego our needs and desires for sexual expression or sexual satisfaction just because we live alone or are single. If we are physically well and emotionally healthy, we want intimacy and physical contact with others. It is a myth to assume, however, as some do, that an active sexual life will take care of all intimacy needs. Similarly, it is unrealistic to expect that marriage will fill every need. Almost everyone is aware of something missing in life. Living alone often means tempering many ordinary reactions and feelings because there is no one to listen or help make sense of them.

For a while in my life, I could not admit to being a sexual being. I could not even think about it because it was such a need. I feared I would rape everyone in sight and sleep with or have sex with anything that moved, including the wives of friends. The message of the church only complicated it for me. I felt shame that I had sexual feelings I could not sublimate. In naming my pain and realizing that it was not only a genital need but needs for touching and holding, I could begin to find ways to distinguish and live with different levels of need.   (Phillip)

Learning to keep alive, emotionally and sexually, is an ongoing challenge for those who live alone. At the very least, it is essential that we recognize and attend to inward responses if we are to stay whole and human. To be human, whether one lives alone or with others, is to be responsive to beauty and joy or respond with frustration, anger, or sadness to the demands and urges of one's body and spirit. Raving to one's self out loud about breath-taking scenery, a delicate rose, or a wonderful new song may be embarrassing to ourselves and others, but it has the effect of keeping spontaneity alive. Taking the time to note what one is feeling can also lead to gratitude for being alive and in contact with the rich gifts bestowed on us by our Creator. It does not, however, settle the dilemmas of being sexual and living alone.

The human need for sexual gratification is fundamental. People respond to that need in a wide variety of ways. Among them are making love, masturbating, hugging and other appropriate touching, dancing, playing with children, finding pleasure in textiles, pottery, or growing plants, in music, art, or the exuberance of the young as they lead cheers or throw themselves into sports. Some of these responses to the human need for sexual expression may be more or less appropriate for the variety of people who live alone. Those who hold the view that sexual intercourse is a personal and private act always appropriate between consenting adults will insist that respecting another's person and body is sufficient moral criteria. Similarly, masturbation begins with respecting one's own body. It is the position of most faith communities, however, that sexual intercourse belongs to the covenant of marriage, which has both personal and social dimensions.

Everyone, to live as a whole person, must attend to his or her sexual and sensual self. What people choose to do to fulfill those needs will be determined by their personal values and religious convictions. If one decides, for personal or religious reasons, not to be sexually active in a genital way, it does not help to ignore what is missing. In his book, *A Whole New Life,* Reynolds Price gives advice to those who are missing something in their lives.[6] He pushes himself and his readers to accept that no one is what they once were or what they wanted to be—a necessary step in becoming the person they will be. If we are not going to have intercourse or be kissed and held and caressed on a regular basis, even if there is no one to wipe away our tears or assure us in the night that what we fear is either not likely to happen or if it does, it can be endured, we can still risk falling apart with joy or sadness often enough to keep those parts of ourselves in working order. Most of all, we need to practice vulnerability often enough to stay attuned to the limits of being human and thereby glorify the God who created us as such.

Facing the older years
and the end of life

Over and over again, from those who have always lived alone and those who are doing it only in their later years, we hear expressed the fear of being unwell and dying alone. There are some people, of course, who would rather *be alone* when they are sick as long as someone is nearby to attend to their needs. While it is true that we will all die and that ultimately, we die alone, the circumstances of our last days are hard to ignore. The prospect of facing our own death is sometimes brought on by a dangerous illness or an accident early in life that makes us look at death for what it is and what it means to us. But even when that happens and life goes on, the question of leaving this life alone and uncared for surfaces with more frequency as the years pile up and reality about one's capacities and limitations are harder to set aside.

> I was telling some friends that I cut my foot when a glass bottle of shampoo slipped from my hand in the shower. It shattered and I stepped on a fragment. Very quickly, the tub and shower looked like a blood bath. My friends asked if I fainted. My response was, "No way; I had to hold myself together in order to pick up the pieces." Fainting is not an option. Because I live alone, I could not count on anyone to take care of the mess. I made it and I cleaned it up.
>
> (Elvira)

> I am quite happy living alone now but I do wonder about what will happen to me when I grow old and am unable to care for myself. With no close family, no children to call on, how will I deal with my house, my property, my care? The prospect is so grim and unclear that I just keep trying to put it out of my mind but, of course, that's impossible. (Cynthia)

Elvira's story is an ordinary dilemma. It calls to our attention, however, that as more and more people live alone and as medical care becomes increasingly outpatient, people will be expected to take care of themselves. Sometimes, the outpatient treatment will make that task very difficult. Cynthia's inability to look hard at the circumstances of her life and her envy of others make it difficult to assess her situation accurately. If one is married, it can be expected that one spouse will die before the other. Even if one has children, there is no guarantee that children will survive or, if they do, there is no certainty that they will have the inclination or life circumstances to "take you in" when one is no longer able to take care of oneself. Housemates and close friends are likewise no guarantee that regular, caring help will be available from them. The implication for everyone is that we need to make decisions for our future when we can. It may be awkward, for example, when both spouses are alive to examine what needs to happen if one dies and the other lives alone. Important information about our lives, possessions, and wishes need to be available to whomever will make decisions on our behalf or take the responsibility for "wrapping up" our lives.

Since no one, single or married, knows the hour of their last illness or death, preparation should be made when all is well, when we can think and decide and get counsel and organize. Preparation is a gift we can leave to those who will attend to matters after our death, whether they are relatives, friends, or legally appointed representatives. Such advance planning makes it easier to cut ties with this life, that we may go more freely and expectantly into the next. For those with the financial resources to do it, arranging for living in a care facility of one kind or another can relieve some of the anxiety, although *when* to make those arrangements is not easily settled. Having a will and a document expressing our wishes for end-of-life care and regarding the prolongation of life in the case of illness or the debilitating effects of having lived so long are also a part of the gift we can give to others.

The Gift of Living Alone

Christian people consider their existence to be a gift from God. The skills, abilities, sensitivities, experiences of all our lives are additional gifts, given by God, for the common good. Living alone and being single is a particular gift that allows people to be and do what those who live with others find more difficult, if not impossible. It is a challenge for those who live alone, however, to see life as a gift to be received with gratitude.

The gift of living alone can be expressed in different ways. For some it will mean hospitality of home or time and spirit. It may mean creating a space in your home, your work, your leisure, or your heart for those who need to be "taken in" and cared for. Caring may be listening, feeding, or providing warmth, comfort, or safe space. It could mean buying two flowers: one for someone who needs a reminder that she or he is known and cared about and the other for oneself—who needs to know the same thing. Hospitality will take some of us to work as tutors with children, as visitors in nursing homes or hospitals, as servers in a soup kitchen, or as greeters at church. The usefulness of the gift in any of these ways is not diminished if, in the giving, one discovers that doing for others becomes a gift for oneself as well.

All children, related or not, benefit from loving, authentic, encouraging, appreciating adult friends. At the same time, every adult should have at least one friend who is a child in order to see the world more clearly and remember more regularly the childness we never outgrow. Children are not the only people who may benefit from the gifts of those who live alone. There are elderly, ill, confused, oppressed, poor, and lonely people; people who are homebound, those paralyzed by fear, people who call out for companionship and for assurance that they are not alone or abandoned. Companionship may come in visits, letters, phone calls, the Internet, advocacy on their behalf, small gifts that alleviate whatever they suffer from or at least make their existence more colorful or more comfortable.

As gift, living alone will not be expressed by everyone in the same way. The ways the gift is expressed will be shaped by location, occupation, energy level, physical capacities, previous experiences, personality, financial resources, and other responsibilities. Some will want to and be able to reach out to many, others will find one or two with whom they can share some part of their life. Some will read books together, others will share a video, some will shop, others will travel to a store or church or on vacation, some will have pen pals and some will be a secret contributor of food, flowers, or notes. Some will join groups working for relief of particular inhumane conditions, and others will join those who pray for God's mercy and blessing on behalf of others. Everyone who lives alone, however, needs to balance giving to others and caring for themselves.

Living alone, when viewed as gift, does not make certain hours of the day or night less lonely. Nor does it provide for someone to listen to or to share in your joys and sorrows. It does not take away those agonizing times when one feels that no one knows or cares. Nor is the gift of living alone a substitute for unfulfilled dreams. Understanding living alone as gift helps the individual see it as a good way to be alive. When people have to give up chocolate for health reasons, they are encouraged to try carob but admonished not to think of carob as a substitute for chocolate. It is a new food in its own right. Living alone as a single person is not a substitute for marriage and family. It is a gift from God—an appropriate way in its own right for some to live with integrity and purpose, even joy and fulfillment.

4

SPECIAL SITUATIONS OF LIVING ALONE

WHEN A CENSUS is taken that determines, among other
things, the number of single households, people who are
married but temporarily living alone are not included in the
category. There are, however, a growing number of people who are
married but live alone occasionally, temporarily, or permanently for
personal, occupational, or medical reasons. By including this circumstance under the heading of living alone, we extend the meaning of the
term beyond its ordinary usage. Married couples are separated for short
or long periods of time for a variety of reasons, some voluntary, others
involuntary. Although these people are married, their subjective experience is more like those who are single and live alone. The spouse who
lives apart is not included in many, maybe even most, of the daily decisions they must make. Because it is an awkward situation to identify
or describe, they are often overlooked when considering the needs of
living alone.

This is not an altogether new phenomenon. In some cultures and
for some classes, long separations between husbands and wives are expected and acceptable. Historically, men have left for work or study
somewhere else, leaving their wives and children behind. Military families in all cultures expect more or less extended separations. For those
who have a summer home, mothers often take their children to the summer home, leaving father home alone until he can join the family for a
holiday. It has also been normal to expect that truck drivers, airline pi-
lots, seasonal agricultural or construction workers, or seamen would be
away from home for extended periods of time. Separation, as such, is
not new. What is new is the frequency, variety, permanency, and the

reality that these separations are now often precipitated by the demands of a wife's work.

—Both Judy and I have a Ph.D. in philosophy. When we married, neither of us expected that it would be so difficult to get jobs that would allow us to live together. It now looks like a commuter marriage is a permanent arrangement. If we cannot ever work and live in the same place, we will not have children.

—I have been alone several times while my husband was on ship for an extended military tour of duty. Every time he goes away I make a list of things to do, some of which I like to do and he does not. Planning helps fill the time but I still waste a lot of time waiting for him to come back.

—My husband has been in prison for nine years. I lived with his parents for a while until they asked me to leave. They thought I spent too much time out with my friends. Now I live alone and I spend even more time with my friends.

—When Jack and Bernadette asked me to preside at their wedding, the request included a confession. Bernadette had been a widow for ten years. Jack's wife had died five months before after living six years with an inoperable brain tumor that eliminated her memory and voluntary motor functioning. The confession was that Jack and Bernadette have had a significant and sustaining relationship during the last four years of Jack's life with Bernadette. "Will you still marry us," they ask?

—After my husband's accident, I found myself making more and more daily decisions that did not include him. I finally decided that since I already lived alone, I might as well get divorced.

—My wife Phoebe has been in a nursing home for four years. I visit her every day even though she has not known who I am for a long time. About a year ago, I started seeing a woman who was divorced after a difficult marriage. It is the kind of warm and loving relationship I need, but some of my friends don't think so.

—My husband and I have lived apart for eight months while I have tried to sell the house. For a while, I enjoyed the freedom, but now I am lonely. I love to bake, but the ginger snap cookies get stale before I can finish eating them. I usually don't tell my husband about all the time I spend with the friends we had made before he left because it makes him sad and jealous. He is waiting until I get there for his life to start.

—When Shirley was called for jury duty, neither of us expected that the panel would be sequestered throughout the entire high-profile trial. What I learned how to do, because I lived alone for those seven months, meant renegotiating some long-standing patterns in our marriage when the trial was over.

—My cousin Pedro is an illegal alien from Mexico who is not only separated from his wife and family; he lives in secret. I know his wife feels abandoned, and he is desperately lonely.

Each situation of living alone, in this subjective sense, evokes a particular response. Expectations of the marital bond are regularly challenged by a lengthy separation. So is self-understanding. Much of what has been written in the two preceding chapters is applicable to these special situations as well. Our aim in this chapter is to present these situations as descriptively as possible to expand our awareness of the variety of circumstances in which people live alone, even for a short time. The content of this chapter is suggestive more than definitive. It is an area in which much more research is needed.

Temporarily Living Apart: Selling the House

Perhaps the most common experience of spouses being separated and temporarily living alone occurs when a move is made and a house does not sell immediately. When one spouse accepts a job in another town or another part of the city, more often than not one spouse must remain to prepare the house and sell it. When there are no children who must also stay behind to finish school or a sports activity, the person who remains for that indefinite period of time lives alone in this subjective sense. So does the other partner, but a new job, new life, and new friends often occupy his or her time more fully. People who have been left behind to sell the house may initially delight in the new freedom. Moreover, because there is often so much to do with the house, they initially have little time to be lonely.

While Hank was getting established in his new job, and, not incidentally, trying to discover if this was where he could build a career, I stayed behind to sell the house. To begin with, we talked by phone every night. As the weeks passed, we talked less and I dreamed more. I made a thousand plans of what we would do when the house sold. For me, waiting for the house to sell was like treading water. When we finally got back together, I was eager to live again. In the meantime, Hank had made new friends, established an exercise routine, found a church, and discovered that he liked his job very, very much. I was hurt because of what he had done without me and disappointed that our reunion did not match my dreams of it. It was a very bumpy marriage for some time.   (Pamela)

Pamela's story introduces a major theme for those who live alone temporarily. While she tried to sell the house, Pamela's life became an extended "holding pattern" in which she waited to be reunited with Hank so that life could begin again. For her, the present was emptied of meaning and the future crammed with more expectations than could ever be fulfilled. By contrast, Hank had not waited for his new life to begin until Pamela arrived. When living alone is a temporary experience, one response is to fill the future with expectation and overlook the present as an empty time filled only with waiting. This is particularly common when a marriage is the primary source of emotional, intellectual, and social support for both spouses. In such situations, the crisis occurs when the reunion cannot match the expectations that covered the pains of being separated.

Long-Distance
Relationships/Commuter Marriages

In a sense, traditional families in which the husband/father was a traveling salesman were the prelude to modern long-distance relationships. Those couples had to make adjustments in their family patterns, but in reality they were together two days every week. As long as the marital relationship was defined in traditional role categories of male dominance, this work pattern would have been occasionally disruptive but the marital bond remained basically the same. Mothers and children or wives alone did what they needed to do during the week, but serious discipline or major decisions waited for father's return.

Byron took a job in Philadelphia shortly before our sons graduated from high school. He left Sunday night and usually came home late Thursday night every other weekend. Our life continued to be centered in Chicago. The family routines did not change until the boys left for college. Then I began rearranging the house to suit my patterns of living. I realized that I could not live my life waiting for Byron's Thursday returns. It took him a while to accept the fact that he could not control those changes because most of the time, I lived alone in the house. It has taken us several years to make this adjustment. Eventually, we learned how to use the time together without berating each other for the time apart. (Fran)

This story is a slight variation on the old pattern. What is familiar about Fran's story is the recognition that marriages that survive evolve a workable balance between intimacy and distance, between focus on separation and focus on togetherness. Some thrive on some distance in a marriage because it limits intimacy, maximizes independence, but still provides for an enduring bond of affection and support. What is different about Fran's story is that she made changes for the sake of her living between the times that did not necessarily include Byron. For Fran, the assumption seems to be that she lives alone except when Byron returns from Philadelphia for a weekend together.

A long-distance relationship often prompts people to value the time they have together. Concentrated time together, some will say, is better than occasional moments of intimacy on the run or when everyone is tired at the end of the day. Having a long-distance relationship, however, is a risky thing. As a friend of ours once said, it is something like regularly crossing a bridge you know may one day collapse beneath you. "My life was so full and rewarding while we were apart," she once observed, "that I realized there was no point in us being together." Because this kind of living alone is so new, we do not yet know all of its possibilities and pitfalls.

The most common pattern of long-distance relationships is generally referred to as a *commuter marriage*. Both partners in such a marriage or a significant relationship work and live more or less permanently in different cities and see one another only periodically. Especially when there are no children, both spouses travel to maintain some sense of being married in two places. In the academic world, this separation is softened by extensive holiday vacations and lengthy time together in summers. Sometimes couples will meet regularly in a third place, a home they have in common, in order that no one feels that they sacrifice the most or do not get "equal married time" where they live and work.

My husband teaches biology at a college in Washington state, and I have been the principal of an elementary school in San Francisco for five years. To complicate things even further,

Peder is from the Netherlands and returns often to be with an aging mother. We meet as often as we can at our summer home in Mendocino, California. We have lived over seven years in small furnished apartments or rooms in residential hotels. When Peder was sick for a year with a chronically recurring virus, I decided to be done with airport delays, commuting through rain and fog, and turbulent flights. I moved to Washington. In retrospect, the illness was fortuitous. I did not regard my decision as an accommodation. It was for my personal health as well as the well-being of our marriage. It would not have endured the commute much longer.   (Meredith)

The commuting style of marriage is a complex, though sometimes necessary, way to integrate career and family living. Commuter marriages usually work best for couples who have strong career motivation and are independent or self-reliant as individuals. It is, therefore, not for everyone, since "people who live apart from their spouses have to be independent and trusting; they must be resourceful and capable of tolerating separations."[1] These separations, whether temporary or extended, are inevitable in an economy that still assumes each worker is unencumbered by other obligations and a family environment in which women and men are each free to explore fully their interests and gifts.

Justice is a major issue in modern marriage. It is also a prime motivator of commuter marriages. The aim is to establish and maintain relationships that are equitable enough so that no spouse is assumed to be the primary accommodator. Modern marriage is complex in part because, for the sake of justice between women and men, it can no longer be assumed that women will do the sacrificing. If, however, the language of rights is used to settle where and how people live together in marriage, the issue is often too quickly polarized. Emphasis on equal regard keeps alive the principle that no one's rights predominate, but it does not assume that sacrifice is unavoidable. The decisions modern married couples must make requires the ability to reflect justly on the demands of marriage, family, career, where and how they live, as well as their obligations toward aging parents. The commitment to justice in marriage today means that sacrifice is unavoidable even though it must be mutual over the long haul.

Insisting on justice and assuming that reasonable people can decide to do what is prudent and necessary may not always fit easily with a parallel need to promote intimacy for the sake of affectional bonds.

The choices couples must make in commuter marriages in support of the affectional bond are a moral problem as well. Separation per se is not the primary problem. In fact, allowing voluntary separation that enhances the career of a spouse may be a generous gift of love. So also, claiming the freedom to develop one's gifts fully that may necessitate a commuter marriage is an action seeking for justice. The paradoxical link between autonomy and community, separation and togetherness is enriched by connecting bonds of affection with justice in relationships.

Separation Without Expectation of Return

Alzheimer's disease is perhaps the most dramatic and poignant experience of living alone in this subjective sense. As long as couples are able to live together, the spouse with Alzheimer's disease is physically present and yet not *able to be involved consistently in the ordinary and extraordinary decisions of daily living*. The emotional separation is particularly painful because it is often prolonged and inevitably permanent. Eventually, when home care is no longer possible, the spouse with Alzheimer's disease must be put in a permanent care facility. That decision is not less painful because it is necessary. The following story, told in some detail, illustrates the agony of Alzheimer's and a courageous way of responding. Harold and Neva Vogelar determined together not to hide her disease and their struggles from their friends or his colleagues. We are very grateful for their willingness to include his reflections in this book.

> My wife, Neva, graduated *magna cum laude* from college. She majored in speech and drama and became one of the nation's leading college debaters. She was, and maybe still is, a brilliant person. Alzheimer's disease is changing all of that.
>
> The children were the first to notice something different—about seven years ago when we first returned from Cairo, Egypt. Neva was inordinately dependent on me and had difficulty adjusting to new things. About three years ago, she became so anxious I thought she would have a breakdown. She had extensive neurological testing and an intensive psychological evaluation. I was never told the results of the evaluation. The doctor claimed that Neva made her swear she would not tell me what it contained. When I finally saw it less than a year ago, I understood why. The report said she may be in the

early stages of Alzheimer's. When I finally learned of it, the disease was too far advanced for Neva to participate in experimental drug testing.

In the meantime, knowing only that something was wrong with Neva, we tried various kinds of medication and psychological counseling. Improvement was promised but did not come. She got lost a mile away from home and told the police she was in another state. Traveling back to Chicago from her brother's funeral, she became completely disoriented and insisted that I was not taking her home. Early last fall, she went into a second bedroom in the night, insisting it was not proper to sleep with a stranger. We finally updated our wills and Neva signed documents giving me durable power of attorney for her in matters of health and property. Late last fall, we had a long talk and decided to tell friends and colleagues. I am so glad we did that because of the support we have received and might not have received had we kept the disease a secret.

Ever since Neva was diagnosed with Alzheimer's, we knew the time would come for final good-byes before memory faded completely. I kept looking for that moment of opportunity before the mind wanders off forever, before lucidity departs, and haziness descends, that point in time that precedes, not the momentary absence of presence, but the final presence of absence. Some months ago, we felt that time had come, and so, amidst tears of joy and sadness, we bid each other our fond and final farewells, just in case. I was reminded in the moment of a verse from Shakespeare's *Julius Caesar,* words that helped us through an awkward but significant transition.

Brutus says to Cassius:

> Whether we shall meet again, I know not.
> Therefore, our everlasting farewell take.
> For ever and for ever, farewell, Cassius.
> If we do meet again, why, we shall smile;
> If not, why then this parting was well made.

And Cassius responds:

> For ever and for ever, farewell Brutus,
> If we do meet again, we'll smile indeed.
> If not, 'tis true, this parting was well made.

(From Act V, Scene 1)

I am happy to report that since that time, Neva and I have shared many smiles.

(Harold and Neva Vogelar)

This story identifies in a powerful way the need to say good-bye "before the mind wanders off forever." It is a fragile moment of final farewell, said with the awareness that there may be other opportunities to say good-bye. If not, at least one parting was well made, as Brutus puts it. The freedom to say farewell depends on acknowledging that some diseases, like Alzheimer's, lead to "the presence of absence." Denying that the loss of mind and memory is inexorable and inevitable or being stoic about the anguish that such a loss generates makes it more difficult to say good-bye. Saying good-bye also means waiting for an appropriate moment. Precipitous farewells are the occasion for melancholy rather than closure and healing. The need to say good-bye comes out of our awareness that we have been loaned to each other for only a short while.

> O Divine Parent and Gift-giver,
> let me not take those I love for granted,
> failing to remember
> that you have only loaned them to me
> for a very short while.   (Aztec Prayer to God)

The response of each family to the crisis of Alzheimer's disease will be unique, determined by the emotional resources available, the legacy of loss each family has internalized from its origins, and the willingness to seek help from outside. All the struggles that come as this disease runs its course will be made lighter if good-byes can be said before it is too late. When a spouse or the family is no longer capable of caring for the person with a mentally or physically debilitating disease, having said good-bye already could mean that putting someone in an institution for care is less like abandonment. Saying good-bye also helps to create the kind of emotional distance necessary to care for the primary caregiver, whether spouse or parent, who lives daily in "the presence of absence." Saying good-bye should also make it easier for the spouse who lives alone in this subjective sense to make his or own plans for present living.

My wife suffered with Alzheimer's disease during the last six years of her life. I took care of her at home and gradually learned to cook and keep house. I miss her presence even though she did not know who I was for a long time. I have done well living alone after she died because I already had some practice at it. I keep busy now as a Hospice volunteer, relieving caregivers of terminally ill spouses or family members.

(Otto)

Living with a person with Alzheimer's disease raises complex questions for the caregiving spouse. When is it appropriate to develop a life alone that maybe cannot or does not include a spouse who still lives? Should the "healthy" spouse begin a life of her own apart from the one who is separated and institutionalized? If the mental illness is serious, how long does a person wait before deciding to "get on with my life?" If a spouse is an invalid, when is it appropriate for the other spouse to begin to develop a social life quite separate from the invalid spouse? Sometimes, it is the sick one who ends up living alone and abandoned. These are critical questions for which there are not simple answers. Caring for oneself while caring for others requires making complicated moral judgments that balance love for the other and the needs of the other with love of self.

The Christian's understanding of time helps in making these decisions. Every human moment includes the three modes of time—past, present, and future—even though one mode of temporality may dominate. We have already identified how living in the future during a period of separation creates impossible expectations but also renders the present empty. For the person with Alzheimer's disease, there is no past or future—only the present. Family and friends live for moments of lucidity in the present without any expectation for the future. Caring for someone with Alzheimer's is a reminder that we always live in the present even as we plan for the future. How we live in the present, especially in situations of temporary separation, determines how we will be able to live into the future.

Prolonged Separation
with Expectation of Return

Under this one heading, we include situations of separation in which there is a definite time when the separated spouse will return *and* situations when the return time is less fixed or cannot be determined at all. Temporary overseas duty in the military, often referred to as TDY, is a regular experience of separation for which the return is more or less determined in advance. Journalists, jurists, attorneys trying a case, construction workers, and people downsized from a job who have found temporary work elsewhere face work assignments that take people away for a limited time, with an undetermined point of return.

I joined the Air Force because I want to work with AWACS. AWACS are the flying radar tracking command centers that are used overseas to monitor and coordinate military air traffic in trouble spots around the world. I decided I would not marry because I knew it would be difficult to maintain a relationship if I was absent for a three-month tour two or three times a year. However, on a visit home to my parents, I met an old high school girlfriend and eventually we were married. I told her that my particular job in the military required long separations. I thought she had accepted the situation. When I returned from Bosnia on my first TDY assignment after we had married, Carla had left, leaving only a note saying that she could not handle this marriage arrangement. I looked for her but never found her. It was an experience of abandonment. I became depressed and suicidal. Eventually I was discharged from the service.   (Manuel)

Even when there is a fixed time of return, living alone is more than some people can endure. Sometimes, as in the case of Carla, we cannot know in advance how we will respond to waiting, even for a fixed return. Other situations of separation may add dimensions of indeterminacy to waiting. If someone is held hostage or hospitalized for mental illness, the time of return is not known. This same dynamic of waiting for some indeterminate future moment of release or healing is operative also when one spouse is in a coma because of an illness or accident. There is a long wait for the return of consciousness. What both circumstances of separation have in common is the experience of waiting.

My father was drafted into the Army during World War II shortly after my parents married. Toward the end of that same year, he was sent to Greece. For three and a half years, my mother heard nothing from him or about him. She lived alone, kept two jobs to support herself, and waited. She presumed him dead. When the war was over, my mother and his family learned that my father had fought with the Germans in Italy until he was discovered to be an American and was put in a Nazi prison camp. Even after he returned home after being gone for four years, my mother's doubts outweighed the joy of his return. Questions about what actually happened to him remained. It took a year before they lived together again. My mother always said, "If the ground is not solid, the house will collapse." My father preferred silence. Before she could promise to be together again in marriage, my mother had to understand what had happened while they lived apart.   (Julian)

Whether the moment of return is known or unknown, there is also anxiety about the time in between. This anxiety is more than mistrust. It recognizes that people are being changed during a time of separation by the experiences of living, even if that living resembles an airport holding pattern. What Julian's story points to in an exaggerated way is the anxiety that couples regularly experience during separation. Until it becomes routine, reentry is always the occasion for some anxiety after being separated. When the separation is lengthy, one or both partners in the relationship may be apprehensive about changes that have occurred in each other or unsettled about sharing space with someone again. Keeping the ground of a marriage solid is an ongoing task during separations and is a permanent dimension of long-distance relationships. It requires trust, the capacity to adapt to change, clear communication, and the recognition that staying married means promising again.

Waiting for Reunion

The dynamic of waiting that is so present in separations because of illness is a dominant motif in almost all instances of temporarily or occasionally living alone. Waiting, as Paul Tillich observed in one of his sermons, "means having and *not* having at the same time."[2] We wait for what we do not have, for what we do not know, for someone who is yet to come, for a future that has not been determined. Waiting means not possessing. In that sense, it is an experience of emptiness in the present. When the separation from spouse, whether temporary or permanent, is experienced as a time of waiting for some future moment to unfold, it is a time of non-possessing.

Waiting is also having. The fact that we wait for something is evidence that in some way we already possess it. Tillich suggests that the one "who waits passionately is already an active power himself. We are stronger when we wait than when we possess."[3] The truth of Tillich's observation is that both waiting and acting are part of the nature of God and human nature at its best. We are no more or less God-like when we wait upon the world or the return of someone we love than when we are working on it and achieving in the world.

Waiting presumes that the future cannot be fixed. It will therefore always be a contingent experience. Waiting is also an experience of caring. A person who views the world with indifference rarely waits. The separation from a spouse or loved one is a time of waiting because the person and the relationship for which one waits matter. When there is not expectation of a return, as with a person with Alzheimer's disease, we wait without hope. That is an experience of waiting on a God hidden in the darkness of an unknown, indeterminate future. One is changed by this kind of waiting, not just by becoming accustomed to the dark, but by seeing in new ways. This waiting without hope, as John S. Dunne has observed, enables us to see more clearly the way God wants us to follow.[4] For that reason, those who wait have gifts to offer to the church. The posture of radical receptivity in our waiting enables us to see and understand in ways that are not possible when we are busy making, achieving, and possessing.

Summary

Living alone, we have said, means being without someone who is consistently involved in the ordinary and extraordinary decisions of daily living. In this chapter we have identified some of the special circumstances in which people who are married or in a permanent relationship may still live alone in an emotional sense. These special circumstances exaggerate the ordinary complexity of balancing the paradox of separateness and togetherness in intimate relationships. Having a spouse with Alzheimer's disease is a particularly poignant instance of emotionally living alone. It is a test of compassion and courage and the commitment to remain until death with a spouse or parent who embodies the "permanent presence of absence."

People in commuter marriages, and other instances of being separated temporarily from a spouse, are caught between the assumption that they share life decisions with someone and the reality that for periods of time that is, in fact, not true. Some decisions can be put on hold until the couple is reunited; others, however, cannot. Decisions that shape one's personal life often must be made as the occasions arise. Although people know this will happen, they are often still hurt by it. Good communication is essential in order to diminish, at least, the element of surprise. Symmetry of expectations also helps. If one partner is waiting to live until the couple is together, as in Pamela's story (71–72), disappointment will surely follow. In the end, trust is the *sine qua non* for people who temporarily or regularly live alone while being married.

5

ALTERNATIVES
TO LONELINESS:
SOLITUDE AND FRIENDSHIP

LONELINESS IS a common human experience. Few people, whether they live alone or live with others, have never known loneliness. It is a central and inevitable fact of human existence. Even people who live in communities surrounded by friends have moments when they feel alone, cut off from those close to them. *Loneliness is what happens within a person when the ordinary and necessary needs for attachment and affection are not met.* It is an experience of being outside looking in, an exile in a place that is called home. Loneliness is aching to be touched or the longing to be heard but afraid that no one will listen or understand. Loneliness occurs when we are isolated from those we love by secrets. It is feeling of not belonging even when we do.

Because the experience often evokes fear and anxiety, we do not always remember loneliness as such. We associate being lonely with walking on a foreign city street at night in the fog, the howl of wind off the mountain and through the trees, the terror of abandonment in discovering that one has been tricked into walking alone in the woods at night in search of hidden companions. Because it even takes courage to examine the loneliness of our lives, it is often a silent, unrecognized companion. Although people who live alone are not the only people who experience loneliness, it is a frequent part of their lives. The following statements from people who live alone reflect this theme of loneliness.

—I feel I have adjusted well to the death of my husband except for the loneliness. I usually plan a big party during the month my husband died. It gives me purpose during a difficult time.
—The worst part of living alone is the experience of an empty

house, not hearing her call, and eating alone after sixty years of marriage. I don't believe joining organizations will solve this problem of loneliness.

—I can get through the days but the nights are lonely. What makes it harder for me is that the couples my husband and I socialized with no longer include me.

—Some people need more solitude than others. As early as age five, I realized I could be perfectly content sitting outside by myself thinking. I am lonely sometimes but I would rather be lonely occasionally than lose my freedom for solitude. Perhaps that is why I have never married.

—We have a saying in Sun City West that if you are lonely, it is your own fault. There is so much to do that can keep you busy, that living alone is just a way of life and not a downside.

The experience of loneliness is unique to each individual. It is shaped by personality factors, expectations of life, the nature of a relationship that has been lost, emotional investment in dreams never achieved, and systems of social support. Not everyone who lives alone is lonely. For many people, the freedom to decide about their life without reference to any other person's needs or wishes overrides loneliness. In this culture, people are less likely to identify loneliness with living alone if they treasure solitude or value independence highly.

It is possible to be lonely in a crowd but the pervasiveness of loneliness is linked with living alone. For that reason, there are cultures of the world in which loneliness is less common because people rarely live alone. In those contexts, the person is understood to be a communal being who belongs to a village, tribe, or family. Such cultures are sociocentric in character and formed around the realization that linkage with one's world is inescapable. People are defined by their role or place in a larger social unit. The prospect of being alone or dying alone is diminished because people value relationships more than success, and belonging more than independence. Even when people physically live alone in sociocentric cultures, they are surrounded by a social web of care for protection and support.[1]

Why Are People Lonely?

There are many reasons why loneliness is a common malady of our time. Urbanization is one source. It disrupts family networks and isolates people from familiar social exchange. And the loneliness spawned by the growth of cities is intensified by the isolation of city living. Those who endured the hot Chicago summer of 1995 were reminded for months that it is a terrible thing to die alone, confined to a cheap hotel room or tiny apartment, without friends or family, filled with fear for every strange sound outside the door. For the elderly, poor hearing, failing eyesight, slowed steps and slower minds may compound this loneliness and isolate people from the simple pleasures of human conversation. Limited income has forced still other elderly persons to find housing in neighborhoods that are dangerous, making many of them prisoners in their own apartments.

Loneliness is not just a social dilemma—it is an individual problem as well. Philip Slater begins his classic book *The Pursuit of Loneliness* with a story about a man who went to live in a hut in the forest to escape from the prattle of his neighbors. He was beset by one calamity after another, most of which were caused by his own actions. One night, while he slept with a gun that he hoped would frighten away boys who came to steal from him, he shot off his foot. "The villagers were chastened and saddened by his misfortune and thereafter stayed away from his part of the forest. The man became lonely and cursed the unfriendliness and indifference of his former neighbors."[2] Sometimes people are lonely and unloved because they are so frightened, empty, or needy that they push away the people they want to come close. Like Slater's stranger, some people are lonely and isolated because they are difficult to love.

Loneliness is obviously not restricted to those who live alone. In fact, our most intense moments of loneliness often occur in the midst of circumstances rich with community. People who marry in hopes of eliminating loneliness in their lives may only discover a more painful form of it. Although we are especially interested in reflecting on the alternatives to loneliness for those who live alone, we intend this chapter for anyone who struggles with loneliness, whatever the circumstances of their living. Our focus, however, is on the experience of living alone. Even for those who are fiercely determined to maintain privacy or who cherish their freedom and independence, loneliness is a discomforting companion at one time or another for those who live alone.

The Loneliness
of Living Alone

Loneliness is more than an urban problem or a consequence of being unlovable. It can be a regular companion for anyone who lives alone. As we have already noted, loneliness is an inescapable part of living alone after the loss of a spouse. A silenced voice creates a different kind of quiet than a voice that was never heard. From this perspective, *loneliness is an experience of deprivation, being without the presence of a loved person.* People who told us about living alone were particularly aware of loneliness when the evenings were quiet, when there was no one to talk with at dinner time, or when they wanted, as in the following story, to share something they had heard, read, or seen on TV—and nobody was there to listen.

> My first time living alone in over sixty years of life was when my husband of forty-two years died very suddenly. The daily living, meals, spare time, handling emergencies were all new and at times frustrating. The devastating part, however, was that I had lost my best friend and I had no one to share my thoughts with. I was lonely but it wasn't a loneliness that could be filled by the presence of another. It was a loneliness so deep that it would regularly bring tears and a sense that I could not survive. (Ruth)

The kind of loneliness that we experience when we lose someone we love because of death or divorce is like a wasteland without inhabitants. It is the intensity of this loneliness that is often surprising. There is a deep aching to be held, touched, listened to again by someone who is now gone. Only silence remains. We miss the social network that also ended by the loss of the spouse. Loneliness comes from this kind of deprivation as well. Even when there is relief from a marriage that was hurtful or crippling, the loneliness may be overwhelming. We are surprised by the depth of our attachment to people and/or our own need to be loved. We may create a new social network, but it cannot fill the gap left by the spouse.

There is another kind of *loneliness that is caused more by disappointment than by loss.* Lonely people may long to be held, listened to, or accompanied in good times and in bad times but are afraid to ask. They wish they had friends but are always busy when someone calls. They may long to be invited but are too ashamed to say yes, so they curse the intrusiveness of people. The fear of love and fear of loss combine to foster patterns of living that breed loneliness. Sometimes people who have always lived alone are torn between wanting intimacy, friendship, and love, and the urge to run from it at the same time. Being connected superficially to many people only deepens the pain of this kind of loneliness. People who have always lived alone may have never learned how to ask for what they need. Loneliness is sometimes the result of not learning how to ask for what one needs.

> I did not choose to live alone. It has been primarily prescribed by circumstances. I love my independence but I have missed daily intimacy and not having my own family. As an only child, I often dreamed of belonging to a large family. I was particularly aware of this recently when I was with my two closest friends, both of whom had children who were marrying soon. The talk of the evening was about an experience I would never have, planning a wedding. Our society is still very much couple or family oriented, and that sometimes makes me feel left out.
>
> (Clarissa)

Whether the loneliness is precipitated by actual loss or, as in Clarissa's story, by the loss of dreams, it is intensified by the experience of empty time. Time is the enemy when we are lonely. When people say that they have "time on their hands," they are usually describing a moment of loneliness. In a book titled *Alone in America,* Louise Bernikow chronicles the loneliness of time in this way: "Life became a month of Blue Sundays, days that make people vulnerable to the fantasy that everyone else was with someone and not lonely, that lovers were having brunch and families were having picnics and the world was elsewhere knit together."[3] Boredom often accompanies this sense of empty time. In order to avoid boredom and loneliness, we sometimes engage in frantic activity that ultimately deepens the painful emotional emptiness.

What we call loneliness may begin as an experience of self-depletion or personal emptiness. Because human beings are social creatures, all losses have the power to deplete one's sense of self. Because the self is formed in part by significant relationships that are internalized, the loss of a spouse by death or by divorce will almost unavoidably precipitate some sense of emptiness or poverty of self. Those who have lived with a spouse before living alone may first experience emptiness before loneliness sets in. When someone says "I feel that three-quarters of me is gone," they reflect the kind of self-depletion that often precedes the experience of loneliness. This emptiness need not be a permanent state. The work of grieving a significant loss is in part a process of restoring a self diminished by loss. Sometimes, however, the loss is so damaging that there is not enough self left to rebuild a future or even anticipate the possibility of a different future. When that occurs, what is referred to as loneliness may be more like a chronic condition of emptiness.

The work of restoring a self depleted by the death of a spouse or the end of a marriage is sometimes a long and painful process of claiming a sense of self that had not been achieved before the loss occurred. In order to grow a sense of self or restore an old one damaged by loss, people in grief need dependable personal support that they can lean on temporarily. Lending ego strength is a necessary part of helping someone whose self has been depleted by loss. It is to be done with clear limits to availability, however, so that caregivers do not prematurely fill the emptiness of a depleted self.

This work of restoring a self depleted by death, divorce, or some other kind of relational loss is important because every alternative to loneliness presumes autonomy. The aim is not to eliminate loneliness; it is an inescapable part of being human. Rather, the task is to live without one's life being governed by loneliness. There are, in this regard, three alternatives to loneliness: solitude, friendship, and service. We will consider the first two in this chapter. In the following chapter, about the ministry to and with people who live alone, we will address opportunities for service as an alternative to loneliness. Without a sense of self, however, solitude, friendship, and service are not possible. Even with a sense of self, learning to live beyond loneliness is a difficult and lengthy process.

I am braver.
I am wiser.
I am stronger.
I am healthier in mind and heart.
I am growing to love life and myself.

But sometimes when I decide I no longer need help, I get scared. (Cynthia)

Cynthia's reluctance to accept her own strength is a common response for those who are recovering from loss. A diminished sense of self is experienced as yet another loss. It is doubly difficult to believe in one's own strength. The guilt of being a survivor and competent is another major impediment to the restoration of a self. Those who survive the loss of a spouse often feel that they are not entitled to happiness in life because the *other* is no longer there. It is even more guilt-inducing if a middle-aged son or daughter is finally free to grow in autonomy or creative freedom because the parent they cared for has finally died. Loss and consequent loneliness are both tragic and full of possibilities. Our loneliness, as Robert E. Neale once observed, "is richer than we know, and, even so, needs to become richer than it is."[4]

Each of the books in this series has, in a variety of ways, addressed the central human paradox of living: the balance between autonomy and community, between being separate and being together. For people who live with others, keeping this paradox in balance frequently requires attention to one's own sense of uniqueness so that each sees the other "whole and against a wide sky," as Rainer Maria Rilke once observed. Similarly, solitude is as much a part of living with others as it is living alone. Solitude and friendship are not mutually exclusive. For people who live alone, friendship is one of the ways to maintain the paradox of communal autonomy even in the midst of solitude.

From Loneliness to Solitude

The word solitude has a rich and diverse history. The words solitude and solitary are both derived from the Latin word *solus,* which means alone. In a religious context, the word has often been equated with the life of a recluse or hermit, someone who withdrew from the distractions of the world into the desert, forest, or mountaintop in order to develop a spiritual life. From this perspective, solitude and society are understood as separate and irreconcilable realities. Moreover, it is very difficult, and maybe even impossible, to move from loneliness to solitude without some kind of withdrawal from a distracting world. William Wordsworth testifies to the healing grace of solitude as refuge from a hurrying world:

> When from our better selves we have too long
> Been parted by the hurrying world, and droop,
> Sick of its business, of its pleasures tired,
> How gracious, how benign is solitude.[5]

There is another way of thinking about solitude, more like our emphasis on the autonomy/community paradox, that understands solitude and society to be interwoven. From this perspective, solitude can be developed and maintained in the center of a big city or alongside an active, productive life. Solitude does not presume melancholic affliction or the desire to escape from the world. In *Reaching Out,* Henri J. M. Nouwen suggested that "when you are alone in an office, a house or an empty waiting room, you can suffer from restless loneliness but also enjoy a quiet solitude."[6] The aim is to be sufficient for oneself and hence not dependent on society to eliminate boredom or overcome melancholy without at the same time being unsociable.

Solitude is therefore not just defined by geography. It is more than traveling from one place to another. Solitude that endures is an inner disposition that does not depend on physical isolation. According to the Roman Catholic mystic Thomas Merton, an individual "becomes a solitary at the moment when, no matter what may be his [or her] surroundings, he [or she] is suddenly aware of an inalienable solitude that will never be anything but solitary. From that moment, solitude is not potential—it is actual."[7] Solitude is one way to be alone but not lonely.

The Journey to the Center: Relational Solitude

The movement from loneliness to solitude is a journey of the heart from sadness and despair to inner peace at the center of one's being. There are at least two different ways to understand solitude that are themselves paradoxically related. The movement from being with others to solitude is *from* the action of relating *to* an awareness of relationship that is not bound by space or time. Solitude, according to Robert E. Neale, is the "discovery of relationships and their existence in our lives."[8] Solitude is the exploration of what is happening or what has happened in relationships. We call this *relational solitude:* talking to ourselves and with others in silence, sorting out relationships, remembering times past, anticipating future meetings, and making peace with old hurts. There are surprising new insights into ourselves and others that occur in moments of relational solitude. The fundamental discovery is that we are not alone in our aloneness. This is the experience the poet May Sarton writes about in *Journal of a Solitude:*

> Today, I feel centered, and time is a friend instead of an old enemy. It was zero this morning. I have a fire burning in my study, yellow roses and mimosa on my desk. There is an atmosphere of festival, of release, in the house. We are one, the house and I, and I am happy to be alone—time to think, time to be. . . . I am here alone for the first time in weeks, to take up my "real" life again at last. That is what is strange—that friends, even passionate love, are not my real life unless there is time alone in which to explore and to discover what is happening or has happened.[9]

This understanding of solitude presupposes an alternation between being with others and being alone. Solitude deepens our life with others by providing time for reflection and exploration of those relationships. Relational solitude depends on the physical presence of others as well as their physical absence. Even when we are present with others, however, solitude, in the sense of being a separate self, enhances the possibility of relationships. For that reason, solitude is not the same as loneliness. It involves neither loss of self nor loss of world. Instead, solitude uses separateness to foster an appreciation of the uniqueness of each relationship and an awareness that we are never alone. The focus of relational solitude is neither self-discovery nor the discovery of the world but establishing the relationship between self and world.

Understanding solitude in terms of fostering relationships benefits everyone. It is particularly helpful, however, for the person who lives alone because it provides a way to be with others even in aloneness. Even so, solitude of this kind is not without risks. Relational solitude not only fosters an interior community, it depends on actual relationships. And those relationships must themselves recognize the value of solitude both for the self and others. This means, as Neale has correctly observed, "giving freedom for the many ways of being alone without being lonely, but most especially with acknowledgment that real solitude can contribute to relationship."[10] Solitude strengthens our awareness of the need for relationship so that we can move from loneliness to friendship as well.

Journey to the Center:
Transcending Solitude

There is another way of solitude that focuses on being with God. This is a variation on relational solitude in the sense that it fosters communion with the Holy One. The contemplative Thomas Merton articulates this position most clearly: "Solitude has to be objective and concrete. It has to be a communion in something greater than the world, as great as Being itself, in order that in its deep peace we may find God."[11] Living alone, from this perspective, is an experience of *transcending solitude*. It is a way of solitude that entrusts oneself to a silence that is beyond all relationships.

The contribution of this approach to solitude for living alone is radically paradoxical. "As soon as you are really alone, you are with God," Merton observes.[12] When we are able to leave behind all relationships in solitude, then it is possible to discover being in God. This contradiction of simultaneously having and not having suggests that solitude is not something we have but a gift one gives. Nor do we possess those relationships that are cherished as part of relational solitude. In this sense, the Christian who lives alone does not use solitude to gain anything, even a higher spirituality. To enter into solitude that is transcending is to accept a gracious invitation to be still, to know and to be known.

Transcending solitude is never a renunciation of community or relationships. Nor is it an expression of contempt for the distractions of the world. We are not to flee to solitude from relationships. Rather, finding God in community will lead both to solitude and gratitude: for the goodness of others, the goodness of all creation, even the goodness of one's own being. We cannot live alone without filling that solitary life with past and present relationships. But yet, insists Merton, "when we act according to grace, our actions are not ours alone, they belong to God."[13] When we find our being in God, we live with a solitude of the heart.

When we live with a solitude of the heart, we can attend to the words and worlds of others. By contrast, if we are lonely, we tend to select just those remarks and events that bring satisfaction to our unmet needs.

When we live with a solitude of the heart, we will not experience boredom. It has been suggested that much of what we do is driven by the fear of boredom.

When we live with a solitude of the heart, we are often, though not always, able to transform deep despondency into sweet melancholy. Living with solitude includes a willingness to welcome sadness and melancholy.

When we live with a solitude of the heart, we do not need to resolve all of life's contradictions but live with them.

When we live with a solitude of the heart, we are not diminished even though we are lonely.

According to Merton's understanding of solitude, living alone as a Christian is possible because one's whole life is marked by complete dependence on the hidden mercy of God. All other relationships pale in comparison to living in the presence of God in silence and in solitude. Some people live for God, some people live with God, but those who live in God do not live with others or in themselves. God does all things in them. Merton presents this impossible but necessary paradoxical ideal. Solitude is both relational and transcending. So is friendship. We experience being in God with others, and being with others points to God. This is what is meant when people turn the hymn phrase around and say what a Jesus we have in our friend.

From Loneliness to Friendship

Solitude and friendship are both alternatives to loneliness. Being alone and being with others are also both necessary to develop life in the fullest sense. Each way of being presumes a functioning self and positive relationships. Neale has described the interdependence of these dimensions in a way that is particularly helpful for those who experience loneliness. "If we are lonely, it means that we have been in companionship and will come to a recognition of relationship in solitude. If we are in solitude, it means that we have been lonely and will enter into companionship. And if we are in companionship, we will become lonely. Each condition is an in-between state."[14] Friendship and solitude are paradoxically linked.

> I have been lonely as long as I can remember. In high school, I was often the outsider watching groups to which I could not, or at least did not, belong. As a boy, I had learned how to compete with other boys, not how to relate to them. I married the only friend I ever had, but the marriage did not last. I never understood why the marriage failed except that maybe I expected too much from the relationship. My only friendships now are connected with my business or the health club. I would like to make friends but I don't know how. (Steve)

The movement from loneliness to friendship is seldom a steady line. Even when being lonely is unbearably painful, making and keeping friends is not a simple solution. Friendship takes time, emotional energy, enduring commitments, some social skills, and a willingness to risk. It also presumes a separate or autonomous self. Steve's inability to sustain a marriage with his best friend may have been in part created by inexhaustible neediness. When one person is expected to meet too many needs, the relationship often fails. If friendship is to endure, it must be an act of freedom. In order to have freedom, there must be limits or boundaries. One friendship cannot, and usually does not, answer all our needs.

The need for a friend is particularly acute after the death of a spouse or the end of a marriage. We have already identified loneliness and emptiness as common responses to the loss of a partner. In some cultural contexts, the ordinary loneliness and emptiness of grief is exaggerated by the isolation of the griever by society or by the inability of the griever to make friends. Keith's wife had died suddenly and tragically. His grief for his wife's death was more than he could bear alone. As a result, he sought counseling. He wrote the following paragraph about one year after his wife's death.

> I need a friend. I am not a good friend to have unless someone will stick with the friendship for a long time. I have hidden for such a long time. The really close friends I have are so far from here. Most of them are unhappy too. I am very close to only a few people. Of that number, only Sam lives here. I talk to him a lot but I am afraid he is getting tired of me. Because I am so lonely, I feel that I must make myself available to some individuals who could be my friends but I am afraid they don't want me.   (Keith)

Even if we have not lost a wife or a husband, most of us can identify with some of Keith's feelings. We need friends but we don't know where or how to find them. We may have had such a long history of hiding that we even wonder if we can be a friend. We do not like to acknowledge that we are needy or dependent, so when we finally do allow ourselves to lean on a friend, we tend to go overboard. Then we worry that they will leave us because we make so many demands. Keith had come to the point in his life when he could no longer hide from his loneliness. He needed friends to survive. This urgency to have friends is akin to a comment by Martin Marty in his book *Friendship* that "we have friends, or we are friends, in order that we do not get killed."[15]

> I think every person who lives alone needs at least two friends with whom you can share deepest thoughts, call anytime, tell anything. I have two of these now. They both need me for the same reason I need them. I know from experience, earlier in my life, that living without these confession-mates (if you live by yourself) is difficult and maybe even dangerous. I have been both careful and fortunate in choosing friends.
>
>   (Donovan)

Being and having friends is not optional for anyone: It is necessary for human survival. Donovan's observation that being without friends is living dangerously parallels Martin Marty's bold statement about needing friends so we do not get killed. What is necessary for all humankind is especially significant for those who live alone. *Friendship provides the opportunity to fulfill our communal destiny to be with others while still living alone.* Because we are communal beings, it is natural to want to express our deepest thoughts or feelings to at least one other person. Those who live with others have a marital partner or other available "confession-mate." Those who live alone need friends to hear their stories, celebrate their success, and walk with them out of loneliness. Understood that way, choosing and keeping friends takes on the weightiness of finding a mate.

Understanding Friendship

In the first chapter, a friend was identified as a metaphor for understanding God's being in relationship to humankind. Drawing on the images of God as mother, lover, and friend developed by theologian Sally McFague, we suggested friendship as a way of being with God that honors freedom and promotes inclusivity. The kind of friendship McFague envisions suggests "we are not our own" although "we are not on our own."[16] That is, we do not belong to ourselves and yet, at the same time, we are not left to ourselves. Friendship with God denies possession but defies despair. In that sense, it is like transcending solitude. To be in friendship with God is to live as we were created to live even when we live by ourselves.

Friendship with God is formed in freedom and sustained by a common vision. True friendship allows each one to be as he or she is. Because the basis of friendship is freedom, being God's friend does not limit God's freedom or ours. At the same time, friends exist side by side, absorbed in some common interest or vision for the world. Others may join such a friendship because they share the same vision. Understood this way, friendship is potentially the most inclusive of all relationships. We will return to this in the next chapter when we suggest that the church is a community of friends, one metaphor for the people of God standing side by side with a common faith in God and commitment to care for the world.

We discover other things about being a friend through God's ways with us. We learn about friendship when we understand that God takes us as we are, gives us room and power to change some things, and shows us how to connect with strangers in order to live for them. We learn from our friendship with God how to be trustworthy with those who share hurts and longings without fear of humiliation or punishment. We learn about friendship from human experience and from centuries of reflection on this complex human reality.[17]

Initially, being a friend is quite simple. We choose to be with people simply because we like them. Sometimes it happens quite spontaneously or unexpectedly that people meet and "hit it off" immediately. We choose to be a friend because of who they are and not for what good they may do for us or what we might make of them. In *Reaching Out,* Nouwen describes this first movement of friendship in terms of hospitality and respect for the other.[18] Beyond this first movement toward friendship that makes an hospitable space for the other, we have identified four central characteristics of friendship that are necessary for anyone but particularly relevant for those who live alone: freedom, shared activity, mutuality, and trust.

Friendship Is Formed
out of Freedom

We cannot be coerced to be a friend. Nor can we force someone to be our friend. We do not create friendship by manipulating from a position of need. Friendship is a matter of freely choosing. Establishing a friendship is a voluntary activity that is not necessarily self-conscious. Keeping a friendship going, however, is a matter of choice: At some point we need to decide that we *are* friends as a self-conscious, intentional act. As friendship becomes a more significant sustaining social reality because more people live alone, we may need to find dependable public rituals that will enable those relationships to flourish in freedom.

The following words, written by theologian Dietrich Bonhoeffer from a prison cell during World War II, express the centrality of freedom for making and keeping friends.

> Not from the heavy soil,
> where blood and sex and oath
> rule in their hallowed might,
> where earth itself,
> guarding the primal consecrated order,
> avenges wantonness and madness—
> but from the spirit's choice and free desire,
> needing no oath or legal bond,
> is friend bestowed on friend.[19]

The freedom that is so central in our friendship with God must be present in human friendship as well. All other relationships are ringed with duty, utility, or desire. Friendship is formed in "the spirit's free choice." This dimension of friendship is particularly significant for people who live alone because they value highly their independence and freedom of choice.

Friendships Are Sustained
by Shared Interests

People who are lovers are normally face-to-face in their absorption with each other. Friends, on the other hand, exist side by side, absorbed in some common interest or shared vision. Ralph Waldo Emerson is said to have asked this question about being a friend, "Do you see the same truth? Do you care about the same truth?" It is difficult to keep a friendship alive unless there are shared, common interests and activities. It is not surprising that people who have young children together become lifelong friends. Playing cards, hunting, belonging to the same sorority or fraternity, having the same ornery boss, playing on the same sports team, belonging to the same church, or surviving the same disease or misfortune are activities, interests, and shared experiences that bond people to one another.

> The Women's Board at church has been great for me because *we* do all sorts of service. The women are very supportive. We have retreats and lots of fun, too. The classes I am taking keep me mentally active and introduce me to more people. I also enjoy traveling alone because I meet more new people. I found volunteer work to help me most. (Alice)

> I would not classify myself as a joiner. I have not willingly sought to associate myself with groups or participate in clubs or, now that I am older, join senior citizen groups. Doing things together with people I hardly know has always seemed a little superficial to me. The lack of a partner prevents me from participating in many activities my wife and I used to do together. (Charles)

Stories we have been told about living alone, like those of Alice and Charles, affirm the importance of shared interests but with some qualifications: (1) Common activities may help to fill empty time but they will only diminish loneliness if friendship precedes the shared activity. (2) People who are introverted or shy are less likely to benefit from shared interest. (3) Doing something worthwhile, rather than just activities as such, is sustaining for people who live alone. (4) Organizations are most helpful when they bring together people with a common vision. Artificially organized groups may provide the occasion for people to meet who will later become friends or sustain friendships that already exist, but they are not a substitute for mutual intimacy.

The Mutuality of Needs Met

Friendships that endure are characterized by a mutual dependency that is delicately balanced. Being a friend or having a friend challenges the myth of self-sufficiency widely promoted in this society. That may be one of the reasons why being and having friends is more difficult for men than it is for women. We cannot make it without a company of friends who will

> hear my story (probably several times),
> tell me the truth about myself,
> protect me from myself,
> hold me when I am afraid, and
> celebrate with me when I succeed.

Friends are needs answered. Friendships that endure depend on mutual self-disclosure. When the delicate balance of reciprocal vulnerability is not maintained, friendship is diminished. We all remember times when we had a hunch that something was happening to an individual we thought was a friend—a marriage was in trouble or a job had ended, there was a serious illness in the family or a child was not doing well in school—only to discover after it was over, or even worse, from some other source, what this friend had been going through. It is difficult to maintain a friendship when we are fearful of being known. We do not hide our needs from friends. Because being vulnerable in the presence of another is both essential and risky, people who live alone are careful about sharing their deepest feelings even when they know they must.

I have been very fortunate in finding people who I could trust with my deepest emotions and most unsettling thoughts who in turn would use me for the same thing. I think some people who live alone are heavy users of therapists of all sorts for this purpose, rather than risking vulnerability with a friend. I believe if more people who live alone had friends in which self-disclosure is mutual and reciprocal, the casual use of therapists for confession purposes could be jettisoned.   (Donovan)

A friend is someone who is willing to go with us into the emptiness or darkness of our lives without fear of being captured by it. A friend is someone who fills me up when I am hungry or lonely and warms me when I am cold and afraid. A friend is also someone who supports my need to give to others in acceptable ways. A friend is someone we dare to ask for help, fully expecting a positive response. I am a friend for others when their needs evoke a spontaneous willingness to respond for the sake of their well-being. Having such friends and being such a friend is a matter of maintaining mutuality.

Trusting Friends and Trusting Friendships

The bonding of friends is achieved through trusting. What one expects of a friend, Sallie McFague proposes, "is, above all else, trust: reliability, constancy, loyalty."[20] The sin against a friend is betrayal. In order for friendship to develop in freedom, there must be a bonding of trust and commitment. If there is to be a future for friends, it must be intended and maintained by a trust that continues beyond the present. Trusting friends, as McFague intends it, is not the same as possessing them. Friends that are joined together by a common vision cannot be exclusive. Trusting friendships are by definition inclusive. They are also fragile.

The relationship between friendship and fidelity is complex. Friendship cannot endure without mutual trust, and the expectation is that such trust is permanent. And yet, because friendship is preferential and reciprocal, it will be subject to change. Gilbert C. Meilaender insists that faithful, trusting friendship is a goal "which can be realized only when the friend is loved in God. . . . Life is a journey, a pilgrimage toward that community in which friends love one another in God and time no longer inflicts wounds on friendship."[21] When friends are together in Christ, their relationship is transformed into spiritual friendship. "Spiritual friendships are life together in Christ and their aim is the mutual holiness and sanctification of the friends."[22]

Friendship is hard work. But friends, like daily bread, are also a gift from God. Friendship, ancient theologians have taught, is truly from God, that amid the struggles of this earthly exile, we are comforted with the counsel of friends until we come to God. Friendship is for the meantime. Despite our understanding of friendship as a way of being with God, a human necessity, and a gift from God, few structures are in place to sustain it. *Maintaining friendship requires the art of improvisation.* There are no religious or public rituals by which we declare friendship with one another. Nor is friendship ordinarily renewed with covenants or silver anniversary celebrations. Moreover, there are factors from the culture preventing us from seeking the kind of friendships we need to survive and thrive.

Impediments to Friendship

The factors discouraging friendship are carried in part by cultural patterns of *competitiveness and self-sufficiency*. Being a friend challenges expectations of self-sufficiency and independence because it presumes mutual vulnerability and need. Being dependent on others, according to the stereotype, diminishes freedom. And if being a friend means acknowledging our dependency, then the messages about being independent are counter to having or being a friend. Competitiveness is equally detrimental to friendship because it does not encourage trust. It transforms shared activities into battlegrounds for winning and losing. Although it has been assumed men were socialized to be more competitive than woman, mixing in the marketplace and shifting role expectations mean that competition is an impediment to friendship for both women and men.

Ethicist Paul Wadell has identified *consumerism and radical individualism* as social and cultural factors that sabotage making and keeping friends. "In a consumer society, friends are just another commodity. . . . People formed by a consumerist society easily lack the deeper spiritual resources necessary for friendship, particularly justice, generosity, compassion, availability, and true freedom of spirit."[23] If we believe that what we own is more important than whom we love, we will be less likely to spend the time that is needed to build friendships. The spirit of radical individualism undermines fundamental requirements of friendship: mutual benevolence and a shared good, the strong conviction that each friend wants what is best for the other and will actively work to secure it.

The third impediment from culture is best described by the phrase *the way we live*. That is, "the way we live" diminishes the possibility of friendship. Sometimes we are so busy that we do not have time to maintain friendship. Keeping busy may also be a way of maintaining relationships at a superficial level that only postpones loneliness or despair. Relationships are sustained through shared activities and common interests, but we may need to change "the way we live" to deepen the bonds of friendship. We are not likely to change the way we live to make room for friends until we acknowledge that it teaches us the most fundamental moral value: to care for and genuinely be interested in other people for their own sake.

When the family is always primary or when it is expected that all emotional or relational needs are met within the family, having friends outside can be perceived as an act of disloyalty or hidden criticism of the family. In the past, when families lived more actively in extended units, it was possible, and maybe even unavoidable, to have all or most of one's emotional needs met within the family. Even today, when extended families are more scattered, relatives still become close friends. Many men and not a few women insist that their spouse is their best friend. In such situations, the tragedy of losing a husband or a wife is multiplied. No one is left with whom to mourn the loss or rebuild a life shattered by the loss.

Summary

Throughout this book, we have sought to establish that living alone and living with others are two equally responsible ways of fulfilling the communal destiny of humankind. Whether we live alone or live with others, solitude and friendship are paradoxically linked alternatives to loneliness. As much as we treasure solitude, we understand that our life with others is also linked with our life with God. Similarly, we hold that marriage and friendship are both fulfilling and responsible ways of being with others. The current interest in friendship is not just another variation on narrow self-interest or a private vision of life. Nor is genital intimacy the only way to embody love and human connectedness. In a society in which the number of people living alone is increasing, it is not useful to take sides in favor of one kind of loving or another. We need relationships of reciprocal love that include marriage and family but also press us into new bonds of friendship that draw their energy from mutual affection and are sustained by mutual respect. Marriage will continue to be the primary way that people live with others. As more and more people live alone, however, we need to promote friendship as an alternative way of fulfilling the communal destiny of humankind. In the concluding chapter, we will explore ways to expand and enrich the church's response to those who live alone.

6

ALONE WITH OTHERS
IN CHURCH

THESE ARE complex times. Sometimes, as a way of responding to that complexity in the church, we organize people around common interests or shared life experience and then develop specialized forms of ministry in response to those groups. So, for example, churches have developed worthwhile singles ministries. Other times, when the number of the people of God who gather is small, we shape a generalized ministry based on who we think we are. Both alternatives are necessary and both are flawed. In order to insure that particular persons or groups are not overlooked in its general ministry, thinking and acting in an inclusive way is a matter of ongoing disciplined reflection for the church. This reflection is especially important because single persons and those living alone have not always been accorded full citizenship in the Church.

The church's vision of ministry has always aimed to be inclusive. This inclusivity is reflected in its methods of ministry, the people who minister, and those for whom the ministry is carried out. In order for the ministry of the church to be inclusive, it must be both general and particular, far-reaching and intimate, a comfort and a challenge to those who minister and to those who are the recipients of its ministry. If the ministry of the church is to fulfill this vision of inclusivity, it must be attentive to uniqueness *of any kind* in those who make up the body of Christ. The dramatic growth in ethnic or cultural diversity in this society has heightened the sensitivity of Christian communities to all differences, including diverse patterns of living.

In this volume, we have identified those who live alone as one particular group in order to further the practice of honoring diversity in the church. We all know people who live alone. We work and play, pray and study, eat and rub elbows with them often. Despite this regular contact, however, many people who live alone still feel invisible, isolated and alone, even in the church. One of our aims has been to diminish this sense of isolation by increasing our awareness of their unique needs and gifts through compassionate observation. The experiences of those who live alone have been set forth in order to (a) bring to awareness unacknowledged assumptions about living alone, (b) identify their gifts for ministry, (c) encourage their full participation in the inclusive ministry that belongs to all, and (d) foster a greater awareness of their particular needs.

What the Church Teaches about Living Alone

The church teaches about faithful living in many ways. The explicit curriculum is what the church intends to teach on matters of faith and ways of Christian living. These teachings are evident in sermons, forms of worship, teaching objectives, mission statements, or material presented in stewardship programs. Unfortunately, however, the whole life of the church has not always demonstrated the ideal of inclusivity that it intends to proclaim. That is, the church's explicit curriculum is contradicted by an implicit curriculum expressed through its ways of being. The implicit curriculum is that which surrounds the explicit curriculum: newsletters, bulletin boards, church budget debates, how leaders are chosen, who gets in and who is left out, and the way visitors are welcomed. There is also a hidden curriculum that teaches without words. It is identified by what is missing: what we don't speak of from the pulpit, in the classroom, or at the council table. Because this curriculum is hidden, we seldom learn from it and cannot evaluate it.[1]

What a church does, intending to be inclusive, frequently invalidates what a church says about its inclusivity. Never asking a person who lives alone to lead a class, greet at the door, speak about tithing, provide refreshments for a coffee hour, or join a family recreational outing negate all the explicit words that may have been spoken regarding different but equally valid ways to be faithful disciples. Speaking and preaching about marriage and family life to the exclusion of speaking about living alone is as bad as having said nothing about the former. The following stories illustrate the power of an implicit curriculum to negate the explicit teaching about the inclusivity of the people of God.

> It happens almost every year. Stewardship season arrives, and after many sermons, appeals, some guilt-inducing words, reiteration of the congregation's hopes and commitments for its future ministry, we are told to go home, discuss and pray with the family about our response. I would probably be talking to myself even more than I do already if I followed all the well-meant invitations from the pulpit at stewardship time to discuss with my family. (Wendy)

> I had moved from a small town in the Midwest to a larger city and a larger congregation about the same time the church began to recognize that not everyone was married. Shortly after I arrived, St. Andrew's Church launched a new program for adult fellowship and called it "Pairs and Spares." I did not like being a "spare" and some of my married friends did not want to be regarded as a "pair" without their own identity. The name stuck and I looked for another congregation. (Kevin)

> I understand that the purpose of a wedding is to celebrate marriage. I expect to hear about the special relationship of the marital bond. I do not expect to hear marriage extolled as the only way to live as a child of God. I know single people who won't attend a wedding because they come away feeling invisible at best and depressed about their life. The last wedding I attended was the worst. At age forty-eight, I was pushed *by my friends* into the crowd of young women under thirty eager to catch the bridal bouquet. (Melinda)

> The congregation I belong to has about three hundred members but only three do not have families. Family is not only the basic image of this church, it seems to be the basic unit for everything. I am the only Sunday school teacher who is not married. In the women's group and at the Sunday coffee hour, much of the talk revolves around children and grandchildren. Because every contact with the church reminds me of an emptiness in my life, I am finding more and more reasons not to go to church. (Roberta)

Each of these stories illustrates how the implicit curriculum contradicts what the church proclaims explicitly about living alone. They are all circumstances in which either the expected focus is not on those who live alone or, as with "Pairs and Spares," the hidden attitude toward being single is negative. In the past, one might always assume more uniformity in a specific congregation. The cultural or ethnic background, the marital status, and the values of a particular worshiping community were more similar than different. Ministry could be aimed generally at the broad middle with the expectation that most people would be included.

Not so today. The growing diversity of ethnicity, culture, styles, and circumstances of living makes it more difficult for a congregation to develop an approach to ministry that is inclusive of each particular population. Large parishes will work toward inclusivity by forming interest groups for specific populations and needs. There are activities for young couples with children or without children, groups for professional persons who live alone, parents without partners, and widows or widowers. A congregation or a collection of congregations may be large enough and diverse enough to sustain this kind of specialization. Even though the intent is to foster intimacy in a congregation, particular interest groups are sometimes still isolated from the whole.

Most religious communities are too small to organize themselves around the interests of members. We are writing this chapter with a small-to-medium-size congregation in mind. In these congregations, it is not always possible to form groups that accommodate every interest. Such congregations must learn how to develop their ministries of teaching, preaching, and hospitality in ways that are inclusive of considerable diversity. We understand that the reflections in this chapter regarding those who live alone are paradigmatic for any ministry that seeks to honor unique populations or particular life issues while at the same time attending to the whole community. By "paradigmatic" we mean that our proposals for ministry for those who live alone could also apply to other groups with unique concerns and issues—that is, victims of abuse, grandparents raising children, adult children caring for their aged parents, and so on.

Marks of the Church

This chapter is an exercise in practical theology. Having examined thoroughly situations of living alone, we turn our attention now to the church's response to this growing reality. We are asking two questions: (1) Can the traditional marks of the church be expanded to support a ministry that is more attentive to those who live alone? and (2) Are the metaphors for church inclusive enough? We have organized our discussion around six traditional marks of the church to emphasize that the ministry with and by persons living alone reflects the general purpose of the church. It is not something just in response to their interests or needs, and yet the needs of those who live alone press the church to consider whether its traditional practices are sufficient for a ministry with and by the increasing number of people who live alone. The final aim is to develop new strategies for ministry that are both faithful to the Christian tradition and yet attentive to these particular people. We will return to the second question at the conclusion of the chapter.

This chapter is an exercise in practical theology. *Its aim is to explore how all elements of the church's ministry might be enriched by a deeper awareness of the joys, sorrows, and opportunities of living alone.* Each of the first four volumes in this series has reflected on the implications of a particular family life cycle crisis for some aspect of the church's ministry. *Leaving Home* included some discussion of the pastoral care needs of daughters and sons leaving home as well as the parents who were left. In *Becoming Married,* the emphasis was primarily on ritual. Planning a "wedding that weds" is one way to take seriously the process of forming a marital bond. The ministerial emphasis in *Regarding Children* was both organizational and catechetical. The public commitment to embody a "sanctuary for childhood" also implies a willingness to give public witness to the explicit teaching that the church is a place of safety for children and childhood. The work of *Promising Again* linked care and ritual in the ministry of a congregation with couples at significant times of transition in a marriage.

The call to be God's people is fulfilled when the church gathers to pray and sing, to know God's word proclaimed in words and acts, to study what faithfulness requires, to celebrate and mourn, to enjoy being together. The call to be God's people is also fulfilled when food is collected and distributed, when children are cared for and young people are allowed to explore their world in safety, when people speak out, protest, or work for renewal in the neighborhood and the wider world. Whenever a living community of women and men in a particular place and time claims to be church, it must seek to realize within itself the elements or marks of church in that place without claiming to be the whole church of God.

These elements or marks of the church have evolved from what has proven necessary to its life. For Martin Luther, these marks were in answer to the question "How can an individual know where this Christian, holy people is in the world?" For Luther and the early Lutheran movement, there were seven identifying marks: the Word of God (scriptures), baptism, the Lord's Supper, the promise of forgiveness and reconciliation (the keys), the ministry (mutual consolation), prayer, and suffering.[2] For John Calvin, it was sufficient that the Gospel is preached in conformity with a pure understanding of it and that the sacraments are administered in accordance with the divine word.[3]

The six elements we have identified reflect the kinds of practices that the church's people repeat over and again. They are about ministries of the church, but they also reflect its core identity. Although we have drawn these elements from many sources, we are particularly indebted to a report approved by the 201st General Assembly (1989) of the Presbyterian Church (U.S.A.) entitled *Growing in the Life of Christian Faith*. We have put the following six elements in the gerund form to emphasize their dynamic character: (1) worshiping together, (2) hearing and telling the Christian story, (3) working together to create and sustain community, (4) listening to and suffering with one another, (5) serving the world, and (6) reflecting together about Christian discipleship.[4]

Worshiping Together

Worship is the primary work of God's people when they gather. The forms or ways of worshiping will vary, but the mark is essential. Without worship, there is no church, no community, no purpose, and no mission. Because worship is directed toward God, it eliminates any artificial human divisions in the gathered communities between adults and children, married or single, gay or straight, black or white, people who live alone and people who live with others. Each person approaches God, praises God, gives thanks for God's creative and redemptive work in the world from a level starting place. Before God, we are the same. In relation to one another within a specific worshiping community, however, we are not the same. The differences within and between worshiping communities are often the occasion for exclusion and hurt.

The differences among people within the same worshiping community become apparent when we move from praise to prayers of confession or intercessions for healing or reconciliation. When the general praise of God is replaced by attention to each particular story and every specific need, it is difficult to keep the ground on which we gather level.

And yet when we pray for others, it is especially important that we have listened to the particular needs of particular people. As congregations become more and more diverse, the general prayer of the gathered people will need to be more and more responsive to specific requests and needs without losing sight of our common approach to God.

A community's ritual life is one place where we need to be attentive to what is common for everyone and particular for some. Our common approach to God is not determined by eliminating differences. Rather, it begins by recognizing that Christ acts through the church whenever the gathered community in worship intercedes and prays. Everyone who gathers participates in thanking and blessing God in the name of and on behalf of the whole creation. Since it is through the church that Christ acts, *each* member of a congregation is understood to be instrumental in mediating the grace of Christ.

The ritual life of the church often parallels the life cycle issues of people in families. We have noted before in this series how baptism and marriage rites mark out significant moments in a family's history as well as an individual's life of faith. For those who live alone these ritual moments may be the occasion for a mixture of joy and sorrow. Melinda's story at the beginning of this chapter acknowledges that a wedding may be particularly poignant for the never married. The same may be true for the baptism of a child. The addition of a child to a worshiping community is a great gift and a painful reminder of loss for a community member who has not had a child but always wanted to be a parent.

> One day, in the prayer following an infant baptism, the pastor said, "and as we pray for all the families of the church, we also pray for those who live alone and for those who are family to them. We pray for parents and their children and for all who, having none to call their own, are welcomed and needed for what and who they can be in the lives of many children." I have been divorced since it was determined that my former husband and I could not have any children on our own. No one in the congregation knows that I was ever married. Can you imagine what that prayer meant to me? (Cecile)

The inclusivity of that pastor's prayer transformed that baptismal moment from a narrow family event to a more inclusive community ritual. The truth of Cecile's story could also be incorporated into a wedding homily. Those who are single and live alone have a stake in supporting healthy marriages. Such marriages allow the single person to have close friends who are married, friendships that are not character-ized by game-playing or guarded behavior to avoid sexual misunder-standing. Such marriages allow wives and husbands to have close friends who live alone and who become welcome, trusted, and depend-able additions to the lives of either spouse and the family as a whole.

Strategic Suggestions for Worshiping

—People who live alone should not be excluded from worship leadership positions such as lector, usher, assistant for the dis-tribution of communion, or greeter.

—If greeters are scheduled according to households rather than families or couples, there is less chance of excluding those who live alone.

—It is essential to note occasionally that the rituals of the church or the forms of worship that explicitly correspond to life cycle moments for people who marry and have children may implic-itly convey a message that excludes rather than includes.

—Ushers should be encouraged to avoid asking "Are you alone?" when they meet a person entering church singly.

—Religious communities provide a context to share life experi-ences that need to be recognized and ritualized or at least held in prayer, such as taking a new job, being promoted, moving into a new house, or becoming president of a community board.

Hearing and Telling the Christian Story

The identity of a gathered people of God is shaped by the stories it tells. Telling the story of what God has done and is doing, reading and hearing the scriptures, and remembering the stories of faithful Christians throughout history are traditional acts of the church. It is the very nature of the church not only to proclaim the Word (Jesus) but *to be* a proclamation of that Word. For this reason, we call the church the Body of Christ. The gathered community is the place to tell the stories of God's movement in our lives in the context of hearing and telling the Jesus story. If, however, what we do together in the assembly contra-dicts the explicit proclamation of the Jesus story, then the church's em-bodiment of that Word is compromised.

Every Christian community must be a community that by its very *existence* continuously and constantly proclaims what God has done in Jesus the Christ. Its communal and leadership structures, the charity with which members relate to one another, how it welcomes the stranger or the one who is different, its presence with and impact on its social context will all proclaim the Word before a word is spoken. Even so, the Word must be spoken. Every Christian community must be a community within which the Word (Jesus) as it is witnessed to in scripture and in the authentic life of the Church is proclaimed. The proclamation through words of the story of Jesus clarifies and challenges the lived Word that is proclaimed through the actions and behaviors of a Christian community.

The Christian story is seldom told in its entirety. Although it is the Spirit of God that empowers a community to proclaim the Word, we are always making choices about what to tell, what not to tell, whom to include, and whom to exclude by the stories we tell. Those who have the power to decide what shall be proclaimed need to be challenged regularly to evaluate their own selectivity. The proclamation of the Word is enhanced when it touches the life stories of the hearers. When the hearers are people who live alone, they need to hear in the proclamation of the Word a sustaining promise for their particular life situation.

Preaching has many purposes. Those purposes include proclaiming the Good News of God's love, encouraging the believer, enhancing the community's worship, comforting those who suffer, and challenging the social order. Preaching is also a way of validating the human story. People are validated when they hear their own story told in the biblical stories of the sermon or homily. What is crucial and increasingly challenging is that people from diverse cultures with different living patterns experience explicit validation in the prayers and in the preaching when communities of faith gather.

I am embarrassed that as a person who lives alone, I had never thought about Jesus as a single person living on his own apart from family for the years of his adulthood. I always pictured Jesus surrounded by his disciples. I was stunned one Sunday when my pastor preached about how Jesus was sustained for his daily living in ways that offer help for those who live alone. He had a purpose for his life. Jesus was open to encountering friends and strangers where they were. He knew the importance of prayer. He took delight in the ordinary things

of life like children, lilies, a wedding, meals with friends, stories, sparrows, and donkeys. (Martin)

It is not possible to solve all the human problems that people bring
with them to worship. Nor can we adjudicate every conflict or comfort
every sorrow that preoccupies the hearers of a Sunday sermon. But we
can validate their experience by linking it with the very real human
stories in scripture. The validation Martin experienced on just one
Sunday connected worship and life in a way that sustained him for
faithful living in the weeks that followed. What is required of the
preacher is a willingness to listen to the diverse stories of people and
the courage to speak specifically rather than generically about matters
of faith.

Strategic Suggestions for
Hearing and Telling the Story

—The preacher's task is to illumine the meaning of being human
and the call to discipleship in ways that recognize how life and
faithfulness is configured differently for different people.

—Sermon illustrations and specific petitions prepared for public
worship need to include the joys and struggles of those who live
alone.

—Encourage occasional or regular gatherings of those who live
alone for anything from Bible study to watching a video or reading a book together.

—Courses, retreats, or reading—on the life of the spirit, the disci-
plines of the devotional life, or cultivating the whole person—
can be designed so that they do not exclude anyone.

—Provide a box in the narthex in which people are invited to place
stories from their lives that might be used as sermon illustrations.

—It is necessary that a congregation's diversity is reflected when
sermon reflection groups are formed. In order to embody the inclusivity that is explicitly taught, every congregation must keep
asking if all the voices are being heard.

—The person who lives alone is an instrumental symbol for the
whole church of the aloneness of every person before God. We
are, before God, always "single ones" embodied in a gathered
community.

Working Together to Sustain Community

The church is called into being by the risen Christ. It is therefore not a voluntary organization or a collectivity formed by choice. Each local congregation is wholly the church even though it is not the whole church. The centrality of Jesus gives meaning to everything in Christian community and locates it in continuity with the life, preaching, and death of Jesus.

Christ is the only head of the community; all other leadership is in relationship to Christ and subject to the Gospel of Christ. Fidelity to the presence of Jesus means that the community will recognize the gifts of each member and facilitate the exercise of those gifts. Although their gifts differ, all members are equal because of their relationship with God. As an organism, the church functions to produce growth, enable action, and encourage persistence in the Spirit of Christ. This focus on functioning presumes that Christian communities will be open, and hence, gatherings of the diverse people of God.

This Christocentric focus on the life and ministry of a congregation means that persons living alone cannot ever be excluded from full participation in the Body of Christ. In fact, the presence of persons living alone adds to the rich diversity of a Christian community. The catholicity of Christ's presence in the world is diminished whenever a community of faith limits participation. Hospitality—more than purity and forgiveness, more than discipline—are hallmarks of a Christian community that seeks to encourage everyone in the work each must do and the vocation each must live.

Theologian Philip Hefner has explored this emphasis on the inclusivity of the church using the phrase "*community of belonging without conditions.*" This image of belonging without conditions is particularly important when we remember that the absolute qualification for being a member of the church is that one is a sinner. Our present struggle is to keep our longing for unity balanced with a need to celebrate difference. Diversity, suggests Hefner, "is perceivable only against the backdrop of unity, and unity can be recognized only from within the matrix that is constituted by diversity."[5] This implies that the bonds created and sustained in Christ are qualitatively different from those in society because they include rather than exclude, acknowledge vulnerability more than perfection, and thereby diminish the loneliness and fearfulness.

> I was visiting a large, affluent city church and after morning worship I moved into the coffee hour. A number of people greeted me and made me feel very welcome. A man who identified himself as a deacon in the church stopped to talk to me. I noticed that he kept looking beyond me so I asked if he needed to be with someone else. "No," he said, "I'm just keeping my eye on that man over there. He keeps coming in off the street. He should know by now that this is not a soup kitchen."
>
> (Rosanne)

No one in the congregation, it can be assumed, needed coffee and cookies more than the man off the street. At minimum, this congregation does not embody Hefner's vision of a "community of belonging without conditions." What the community also misses are the gifts that strangers bring. In order to receive the gifts each one brings, we need to practice setting aside our concerns for the sake of others. Giving way to one another in obedience to Christ is not easy, but gospel living is seldom without cost. The practice of "giving way to one another" is necessary, however, if the church's explicit curriculum of belonging without conditions is to be heard.

Strategic Suggestions for Working Together

- Spell out the invitation to everyone when it is appropriate that everyone participate. That is, do not assume that people who live alone will know they are welcome.
- Be attentive to the barriers to participation for those who live alone and seek ways to minimize such barriers as coming alone, transportation, fear of being out at night, and fear that there will be no one familiar enough to talk with.
- Continue to identify those who live alone who are gifted for leadership on the boards and councils of a local community and suggest such individuals for service beyond the local church.
- The challenge for the Christian community is to witness to the communal nature of the life in Christ—which is no easy task for churches that are increasingly seduced into "going it alone" and are apparently unwilling to make the sacrifices that would be called for in interdependent living at the institutional level.
- When there is a church fellowship event for which a fee is charged, it is more inclusive if the cost is always advertised per

person for everyone rather than per couple with some exception for those who live alone.

Listening to and
Suffering with One Another

The work that is done by God's people, gathered for the sake of building up the Body of Christ as community, is balanced by mutual care of one another for the sake of individual growth and development. This mutual care has many expressions. It is manifested in confessing sins to one another in order to be reconciled. Forgiving one another and being forgiven is the way Christians actualize the grace of God in their relationships with each other. Mutual consolation is embodied in the way Christians tolerate one another's failures and celebrate successes. And whenever we enter into the suffering of another person, we enter into the heart of God that groans in travail with us and for us.

A community of believers that gathers with the cross of Jesus Christ at its center does not flee from suffering. In fact, such a faith community is known by the way in which people suffer with and for each other. The church as a community of suffering people continues to embody the presence of the suffering God in the world today. This is our Christian calling because we have been incorporated into Christ's life. This experience of being held by a community of suffering people may in fact be the only answer to the problem of suffering some people ever get or need.

The commitment to listen attentively to one another about the particular experiences of life is the quality of Christian community that is most liberating for those who live alone. If our attentiveness to one another is one of the marks of the church, then listening to one another's stories is not optional. For some who live alone, it may be the *one place they can count on* where their particular stories are heard. For others, the Christian community may provide a context to think through personal decisions or consider complicated options. The community is enriched by hearing the stories of those who, by living alone, are regularly in touch with the gifts of solitude. Listening to and suffering with one another has intrinsic worth because it reflects the message of Jesus to be with one another. It also strengthens individual believers for their ministry in the world.

After years of living alone, I observe that most others like myself fall into one of two extremes when it comes to self-revealing.

> We either talk nonstop about the experiences of our lives whenever anyone will stop long enough to listen, or we find it almost impossible to do so when others share the ordinary joys and difficulties of their lives. The first way seems almost compulsive and is often followed by embarrassment and an apology. The second often reinforces a sense of being a nonperson or a tendency to retreat more and more from any public or social life. (Freda)

One of the gifts of a Christian community is that a committee, class, or fellowship group can provide a structured invitation for people who live alone to speak about their lives. A focused request to tell of an experience of feeling lost, of knowing oneself to be inadequate, or of being aware of God's presence serves both types of people described in Freda's story. People who live alone may not be asked to speak about themselves for weeks. Because of a fear of saying too much or not enough, the invitation to speak of oneself is doubly gracious if it includes a suggested time frame.

Strategic Suggestions for Listening with One Another

—Invite those who live alone to be in prayer for the sick and the grieving or for those activities in the church which need God's leading in serving the needs of people.

—Facilitate occasional gatherings for brunch after Sunday worship or for Thanksgiving/Christmas/Easter dinner or other times when those who live alone may feel that everyone else is with someone.

—Inquire about the needs of those who live alone—like grocery shopping, income tax, moving furniture, putting up a Christmas tree, cleaning up after a storm, or programming a VCR—and connect them with people who are willing and able to help out in those areas.

—Listening to one another is not an idle exercise. Christians have long sensed the importance of narrativity, of the individual composing his or her life in context. Listening identifies the communal context of crafting one's life through "hearing one another into speech," as feminist theologian Nelle Morton once described it.

Serving the World

The church is a community called by God in order to be sent into the world. It is a community that exists for the sake of mission, to continue the saving presence and action of Jesus in every time and place, to proclaim the coming reign of God, to lead by its example as a just and reconciling community, and to serve the whole of humanity.

The Christian community is local and historical. It is located in time and space and therefore characterized by the locality in which it exists and is called to serve. One of the ongoing tasks of the church is to become conscious of, and understand the nature of, the context in which we live. The hospitality shown toward one another in the community is also reflected in a community's response to the stranger at the gate or the needs of a neighborhood.

> I amazed all my friends and myself as well by volunteering for a church mission project in Central America. Arranging for mail to be held, a dog to be cared for, my new address circulated to friends I thought might write, and then deciding what I would need in a place I had never been helped me realize I had taken the biggest risk of my life. I had signed up for six months. No one was more surprised than me when I gave my dog away and signed up for six more months. In that remote and strange place, people needed what I could give and they welcomed me for who I am. I also found new friends in the other volunteers. I will not be the same. (Andrew)

Strategic Suggestions for Serving the World

—Recognize in worship or somewhere in the life of the congregation (bulletin board, etc.) those who serve in organizations in the community or the world that honor the vision of God for all humankind.

—Continue to survey the needs of a particular community and seek to find resources in response to those needs. This does not mean that the church must respond to every need with a new program, but it does mean that the church continues to advocate for those who are discarded, abandoned, or overlooked in society. Those who live alone are frequently among the neglected ones.

—Challenge all people, including those who live alone, to short-
or long-term mission assignments. Those who live alone may
need encouragement to embark on service outside their normal
pattern of careful planning and cautious adventuring.

—The increase in outpatient medicine and the growing number of
people who live alone together present a major dilemma. The
church may serve those who are in outpatient medical treatment
and live alone by providing assistance in such things as changing bandages or doing exercises at home. The "Nurse in the
Parish" program is a voice of advocacy for those who live alone
and have no one to speak for them when they are sick.

Reflecting Together
about Discipleship

This sixth mark of the church is a communal expression of what is
often called theological reflection. There are two foci for this ecclesial
activity. The community is both the context *and* the agent of theological reflection. In one, the community of faith, as community, reflects
on its life together in order to discern the call of God in their midst and
to know best how to respond to the situations that confront them. This
model of theological reflection has been one source of power for base
Christian communities in Latin America as they have sought to remain
faithful to the Gospel in a hostile environment.

The religious community is also a context for individuals to reflect
on their life in the world. Often theological reflection must be done "on
the run" as we sort out the consequences of a difficult ethical dilemma
in the workplace or where we live or play. In those instances, we have
to depend on good habits that have been formed in communities of faith
in order to be a practical Christian, thinking about faithful living in the
world. Each individual point of view, for all its authenticity, needs to
be enriched by others. In that sense, theological reflection is not only
communal, it is also collaborative and dialogical.

The role of the Christian community in providing a context for theological reflection is increasingly important as more and more people
live alone. The family (including a couple without children) is almost
inevitably a community of moral inquiry because of the complex decisions it must make in order to distribute power and yet honor both individual and communal needs justly. It is not possible for Christians who
live in families to avoid making moral choices. They may not always

be made justly—or even if they are just, they may be made unilaterally. Moreover, people who live in families have a community of at least two in which to think through the implications of the choices we make. Such is not the case for those who live alone. They need the church to be a reflecting community in order to help individuals who live alone discern more clearly the intention of God for their life. This need is clearly illustrated in Jayne's transformation of a Bible study group into a community of discernment.

> I belong to a Bible study group in my church that includes both married and single people. We had good discussions, but after meeting for six months I still did not know anybody. I had decided to go back to school but had not determined an area of study. I am not good at getting advice from my parents so I invited the group to my apartment for dessert and coffee. I asked them to identify my strengths and weaknesses and possible areas of study and work. I was amazed that everyone came and participated. I got the help I needed but most of all learned more about the people in my Bible study group. Now everybody consults with the group! (Jayne)

We need others to help us discern our gifts. We also need others to help us criticize and resist those powers and patterns (both within the church and in the world) that damage the human spirit, undermine human community, and thereby injure God's creation. It has always been difficult to be Christian apart from community. Maintaining a Christian vision of responsible living in an increasingly secular society is less and less a solitary task. In response to this challenge, the church needs to be formed as a context in which to examine and promote the things that make and keep life whole. Understanding the church as a community of moral inquiry is a particularly beneficial image for people who live alone.

Ethical Obligations and Living Alone

In the first book of this series, *Leaving Home,* it was suggested that leaving home is an ethical act because it implies discipleship or vocation. Leaving home enables us to discover, foster, and utilize our gifts for ends beyond the meeting of our own particular needs. For that reason, parents have a moral obligation to bless their children and let them go. The second book, *Becoming Married,* considered ways in which justice must be present in order to form a marital bond that endures.

Becoming married is an ethical process because it involves making choices that establish a bond in which the uniqueness of each spouse is recognized and honored by the other.

When children are added to a family, parents are morally obligated to provide protection and nurture. The image of vulnerability was used in the third book, *Regarding Children,* to emphasize the importance of making communities in which it is safe to struggle toward the goal of childhood. The family is also a community of moral inquiry not only because it teaches values but also because of the way it values each member. *Promising Again,* the fourth book in the series, develops the idea that marriages are more likely to endure if couples are able to keep promising to one another. Finding a balance between what we must do, what we could do, and what we would like to do is an ongoing human dilemma.

There are two specific ethical issues for those who live alone that intensify the need for the church to be a community of moral inquiry. The first occurs at the end of life, when one spouse of elderly parents dies and the other is no longer able to live alone. If the surviving spouse is able to live alone, the first adjustments to be made are more social and psychological than ethical. When a surviving parent is no longer able to live alone, however, adult children or the extended family often have complex decisions to make affecting the well-being of a parent and the family as a whole. A supportive community in which to explore options is helpful, especially because decisions about parents are often so emotionally charged.

The second ethical challenge is more a daily dilemma for those who live alone. It is easy to absolutize one's own needs or desires without the presence of another (like a husband or wife) who regularly challenges the human propensity for selfishness. On the other hand, as we have already noted, there are also people who live alone who have difficulty claiming their own needs as appropriate. Those who live alone need the church to be a community of moral inquiry to keep self-sacrifice and self-love in balance. Even when a person living alone is actively involved in a life of faith and appears to be living for others, the struggle between selfishness and selflessness can be a daunting and burdensome one. Open discourse about the dilemma, supported with insights from scripture, church teachings, and the wisdom of other faithful Christians can be a gift. Although each of the transitions and tasks in a family's life cycle has an ethical dimension, the dilemmas of living alone benefit particularly if the church can be a community of moral inquiry.

The Church as a Community of Friends

As we conclude this practical theological consideration of living alone, we return to the questions with which we began. Are the marks of the church, as we have defined them, comprehensive enough for a ministry that seeks to be attentive to the concerns of people who live alone? These characteristic elements of the church, when examined through the lenses of people who live alone, do not preclude inclusivity; they simply need to be expanded. The strategic changes we have proposed regarding the ministries of the church on behalf of those who live alone deepen, rather than eliminate, its fundamental marks.

The metaphors or images we use to speak about the church and its ministry in its horizontal mode need to be expanded, however, as a result of this focused attention on the experiences of living alone. The images used to describe the *vertical dimension of the church* relate, in one way or another, to God's embodiment in the world. The church is in the world but it is from God. Images that reflect this aspect of the church's life emphasize its origins in God. Whether the church is understood as the Body of Christ, the Bride of Christ, or an extension of the Incarnation, the meaning is constant: The church is from Christ and on behalf of Christ for the sake of the world. The church is a community of God's redemptive presence. As such, the church is witness to and embodiment of what God is doing in the world, interpreted in and through Jesus Christ.

The *horizontal dimension to the church* reflects the ways in which the church, as the embodiment of God's presence, is a very human reality. The church is an earthen vessel that is shaped by its culture. It is a human community of ordinary people bound together by shared experiences of faith and life interpreted through the Christian story. For theologian Rebecca Chopp, the emphasis on mutuality and relationality in God and in human nature leads to three fundamental symbols of ecclesia or church: as the counter-public of justice, as the locus for a spirituality of connectedness, and as the community of friends.[6] *This last image of the church, as a community of friends, links our emphasis on the communal nature of human nature with a relational view of God for the sake of a more inclusive image of the church.*

Family metaphors generally dominate images of the horizontal dimension of church. It is common to speak of the church as the Family of God or the Household of God. Gerald Foley, in his book *Family-Centered Church: A New Parish Model*, has taken the family metaphor one step further and suggested, in keeping with the spirit of Vatican II, that the family is the first or maybe even primary church: "A family is our first community and most basic way in which the Lord gathers us, forms us and acts in our world. The early church expressed this truth by calling the Christian family a 'Domestic Church' or 'Church in the Home.' "[7] Either way, family as church or church as family, the dominant metaphor for church is familial.

There is no doubt that religious communities function like family for many people. Moreover, family images or household metaphors are common in the New Testament and early Christian practice. The family metaphor is commonly used whenever we think about the church as an intimate community partly because family is the primary image for reciprocal, intimate relationships. When, however, we look at images of church through the eyes of those who live alone, family images exclude rather than include. While it is undoubtedly true that most everyone belongs to some kind of extended family grouping, it is not the primary, ongoing reality of those who live alone. We need to expand our images of church to provide more ready identification for people living alone. *The church as a community of friends provides that image.*

We have already suggested that being in relationship with others is a fundamental dimension of human nature. Human beings are communal creatures, destined to live in relationship with others. Marriage and family have been and continue to be the most common form of persons-in-relation with others. In our time, however, we have come to acknowledge other ways of living with others that promote human growth and well-being. Living with others is not the only way to fulfill the social dimension of being human. For that reason, we concluded in the first chapter that wholeness is settled not by "with whom we live" but by "the way we live." We have identified interdependence and communality as fundamental themes for Christian anthropology.

Our discussion of God as friend is continued in this image of the church as a community of friends. Jesus, as McFague has observed, "is a parable of God's friendship with us at the most profound level."[8] If God is understood in terms of connection and mutuality, and if our understanding of being human is equally communal and relational, then the church must also be thought of in interdependent and communal ways. Family is one experience of persons-in-relationship. Friendship, however, is another. What that image means for Chopp, and what we intend it to mean for this book, is that the church as a community of friends is "a community of truth-telling, of hope, of nurturing connections."[9] This is deeply tied to an image of church as the place where justice is envisioned and practiced, where belonging is unconditional, and where grace is present in the fullness of all relationships. This image of church as a community of friends united by a common vision of fulfillment for all reflects the longing for inclusivity and for places of belonging without conditions.

There are dramatic changes that have taken place in human ways of living during our time. Among those changes has been the increase in people living alone. At the same time we have come to understand God in more relational ways. These two themes are not mutually exclusive. Friendship, which always recognizes the uniqueness of the other within a bond that honors both equality and mutuality, becomes an appropriate symbol for our relationship with God. Because more people live alone, we also need to think again about both our anthropology and our understanding of church. Attending to the experiences of those who live alone at least reinforces the necessity of adding an image of the church as a community of friends to familial images in order to provide a more inclusive picture of the church and its ministry with people in all circumstances of living.

Epilogue to the Series
Family Living
in Pastoral Perspective

EPILOGUE
THE FUTURE OF FAMILY

THE ENGLISH theologian John Hick once observed that finitude is generally a good thing. The awareness of being finite is also valuable because it enables one to see an experience in its totality. When a vacation, a time of intense work, an academic class, or a romance ends, we can evaluate the vacation or work or class or romance as a whole to determine its value or meaning. The ending of a life is like that. The life review that is often part of dying not only acknowledges finitude, it enhances closure. The end of this series of five books on family living is another occasion when an awareness of finitude generates reflection. All of the authors, with the exception of Kenneth Mitchell, who is deceased, have participated in this review. The spouses of those married have made significant contributions to the epilogue. We found this end-of-a-series review particularly beneficial in identifying critical issues facing the future of family. Our intent has been to present our observations in a way that fosters, rather than polarizes, conversation.

The Future of Family

Not so long ago, it was common to wonder whether the family, as we had come to know it, would survive. The family was regarded by many as an endangered species. Some predicted the collapse of the nuclear family from the weight of more expectations than it could bear. Others declared it would become redundant because many of its former tasks were being taken up by the larger society. Still others worried that the family as an institution could not survive the breakdown of what was understood to be its traditional form. A few people even wondered whether the family *should* survive at all because it restricts developmental freedom or teaches selfishness. Increases in juvenile delinquency, single parenting, underachieving children, violence toward women and children, changing family structures, and role confusion between men and women in marriage have been regarded as sure signs of the family's demise.

Prophecies regarding the family's demise have not come true. What we have learned instead is that the family is a very durable social institution. The model of family living that has emerged is one of diversity and flexibility that in turn produces a kind of controlled disorder that varies in accordance with pressing social and economic needs. Complexities in living patterns, conflicts in roles, and variations imposed on individuals from the demands of modern society require an even greater diversity and malleability. The diversity of forms is not, however, the reason for the family's demise. The form of the family has changed throughout human history and will keep changing. The family has a future in part *because* it keeps changing. And because the family continues to change, it will always be characterized by "a kind of controlled disorder."

What Kind of Family Has a Future?

The future of family may not be what we expect. Even if the family endures, the changes that continue to occur will increase rather than diminish the diversity of structures. We regard the variety in family forms as a sign of health and an expression of God's creative extravagance rather than a sign of decay or evidence that the family is in trouble. Even so, structural diversity makes defining family more difficult. Although family membership is ordinarily determined by marriage, birth, or adoption, there are many other kinds of relationships that people call family. As we continue to expand the range of relationships that function like family, we also need to keep asking how broadly we can define family without eroding its meaning or jeopardizing its purpose.

Optimism about variety in family structures is, however, tempered by the realization that some family forms are better than others for the people who live in them. Most family arrangements can be good enough for survival and growth. Some, however, are not. Determining what is lacking in a particular expression of family requires careful listening to developmental needs, the legacy each nuclear unit has received from its homes of origin, and the resources of its social context.

Establishing universal criteria for an adequate structure is difficult because the purposes and functions, and hence, forms of family, evolve in relation to its larger social contexts. In that sense, family and culture create each other.

The theme of paradox, which has been constant throughout this series, is intended to serve as one check against the tendency to polarize alternatives. One way to keep paradox alive is by continuing to say the other side. If marriage is promoted as the royal road to happiness, it is useful to insist that it is also possible for those who live alone to be happy. So, also, we need to affirm the value of good marriages for the sake of children while recognizing and enhancing the possibility that other family forms also provide the protection and nurture both children *and* adults need to grow and flourish. The question of the future of family is therefore not about its survival. Rather, the question is what kind or forms of families should endure as we move into the future.

What Kind of Future
Will There Be for Families?

The issue of survival is larger than the family. It is about the future of the world as we know it. If we could establish forms and functions that are adaptable enough to insure continuation of family, we would still need to ask about the kind of future we can imagine. Any discussion of the family's future immediately moves to wider and wider circles of public influence. At minimum, the focus on environment includes recognition of the need for policies in business and government and church that are devoted to creating a family-friendly social context. Flexible parental leave time or generous day care are essential, but the family needs more. The broader and deeper issue is about establishing sustainable environments for the future of our children's children.

There is a poster of a woman with a child at a breast that is in the shape of a globe. The caption on the poster expresses in a compelling way an issue for our time: *Our children ask the world of us.* Our deepest ecological passions and our best political wisdom are needed in order to make the world safe for our children and to keep our children safe for their future. In this sense, the future of family is an ecological issue. We need to develop a global way of thinking if there is to be a future for our families. Modest proposals will not do. In order to create an environment safe for the future of all children, there needs to be a fundamental shift in the social agenda, a shift that recognizes a fundamental interdependence between people and environment. A future for family depends on it.

Troubled Families/Troubled Society

The affirmation that the family is a durable institution does not diminish the reality that many individual families are seriously troubled. In some ways, the family is deteriorating. The continued frequency of divorce, the rise in out-of-wedlock births, absent fathers, the growing poverty of divorced or never-married mothers, and the declining mental and physical well-being of some stepfamilies or single-parent families continue to be evidence that the family is in deep trouble and in need of transformation. The decline of the two-parent family, however, is not the primary cause of that crisis. Unfortunately, some of those uncritically committed to preserving family values are at the same time the defenders of a post-industrial free-market economy that puts strain on the ability of families to flourish. Because the family and society are so inextricably linked together, we need to understand that the crisis of the family is a crisis of the society as a whole.

Asking the family to solve this crisis is, in large part, blaming the victim. The crisis is much larger. As long as we continue to focus on rehabilitating the nuclear family, or at least restoring the two-parent family as *the* major issue in our society, then we do not have to address the erosion of the middle class, institutionalized violence, rampant cynicism, the abuse of power at many levels, conspicuous consumerism that traps us in an endless cycle of greed, racism and sexism throughout society—all of which contaminate the environment in which families struggle to survive. These things are the source of our deep and vexing national anxiety. Further, these influences contribute to a devaluation of family by society. The assumption that we can restore family values or the two-parent family without addressing these destabilizing forces in society is wishful thinking and ultimately conterproductive. The family is troubled because society is in trouble. Therefore, reforming the family and reforming society are and must be the same agenda.

Most families are doing the best they can under increasingly stressful circumstances. It is true that there are families that abuse or neglect children. There are families that create such a toxic atmosphere that the well-being of everyone in them is undermined. Sometimes, however, parents are trapped in a cycle of overwork and fatigue, and hence, inattention to children occurs because of choices prescribed by a consumer culture. In order to have a bigger house in a safer neighborhood with better schools, both parents work more, attend to one another and the children less, and thereby foster a poverty of meaning and purpose in the family that is only exaggerated by a bigger house. Even a family with no children but a have-all-you-can-have mentality is robbed of deepened relationships with each other and all others. It is not correct just to blame selfish feminists, parental greed, or absent fathers for this crisis. We have all learned the lessons of consumerism well: work more to spend more. Families caught in this cycle of consumerism need to learn that less is more.

Efforts to Strengthen Marriage

This series of books has been written during a time when new concerns have been expressed about the emergence of a so-called divorce culture and the negative consequence of divorce for children in particular. No-fault divorce laws, aimed at sparing children from bitter battles, made divorce too easy, opponents of the current law argue, and have thereby unwittingly contributed to the feminization of poverty. The time has come, it is said, to shift our attention from divorce to marriage and to rebuild a family culture based on enduring marital relationships. One way to save marriages, as this argument goes, is to make divorce more difficult, at least until children are grown.

Making divorce more difficult is matched by other efforts to make it harder to marry. There has been an effort among some conservative Christian churches to insist on more premarital counseling before the wedding, again with an eye toward saving marriage. Helping people get ready to marry becomes a major focus of the church's marriage ministry. This approach is necessary but not sufficient. If the church intends to strengthen marriage, it needs to provide regular opportunities for couples in their first years to receive competent and ordinary help early in the process of becoming married.

There are many reasons why building marriages that endure is necessary. Concern for children is first. Two parents in a loving and respectful relationship are undoubtedly the best environment for children. Enhancing personal growth and well-being for husbands and wives is second. Social stability is a third reason to keep working toward more effective living in marriage. Getting men to take responsibility for the offspring they procreate not only will improve the lives of children, men, and families, it will help diminish social violence. Proponents of making divorce more difficult have added pragmatic reasons for staying married, like greater personal wealth, better diet and medical care, and less risk-taking behavior in general, all of which contribute to a longer life.

Three themes are missing from this rhetoric in support of marriage that need to be added so that avoiding divorce does not generate more problems than it solves. Pragmatic arguments in support of marriage overlook its spiritual dimension. We mature spiritually when we "stay the course," that is, when we open ourselves through enduring relationships and not just to the pleasure of affection and intimacy. Spiritual maturity also includes the challenges of honest confrontation and confession, forgiveness and reconciliation. We need the experience of fidelity. Marriage is not the only place to experience fidelity, but the world is diminished if it is not one of the places.

It is not easy to stay married. That is the second theme. Our efforts to support marriage cannot overlook the complexities of modern marriage. To those who are single and live alone, there are tax breaks and house benefits that regularly favor those who are married. On the other hand, there are cultural trends that make it difficult to stay married. Radical individualism continues to erode the practice of citizenship; it also diminishes the willingness to make binding commitments of any kind. The freedom to follow personal pursuits, unrealistic expectations of perpetual romance from popular culture, even the larger pattern of buying new rather than repairing the old make staying married countercultural. Given these cultural forces, it is remarkable that many people still marry, stay married, or marry again. We need to be empathic with people who struggle, often under adverse circumstances, to remain in committed relationships. We also need to continue to find ways of being empathic toward people whose marriages do not last even as we seek to strengthen marriages by making divorce more difficult.

Efforts to reclaim the ideal of marital permanence often focus on cultural or legal permission to divorce but tend to overlook what is necessary to stay married. That is the third theme that needs to be added to the current family rhetoric. Becoming married is a process that happens over time. Staying married presumes a commitment to keep promising again and again. Throughout this series we have sought to provide new ways of thinking about becoming and being married that take into account the inevitabilities of change that often destabilize even the best marriages. Although there is not a single blueprint for promising again, marriages that endure welcome the call for change that is deep enough to transform both the marriage itself and the people in it.

Reordering Our Priorities

One source of our present trouble is that neither the traditional nuclear family nor a market-driven society have been able to adjust to the changes in the social roles of women and men. Although more women work outside the home and men assume more responsibility for nurturing children, *expectations of the workplace have not changed*. One of the reasons families are troubled is something that is built into the organization of modern, industrial, market-driven societies: The expectation of the marketplace is that each worker is ultimately a single, unhindered individual, unencumbered by significant relationships, marriage, or family. If that is so, it is not surprising that the family often features a constant juggling act of multiple ambitions and conflicting obligations. A society that rewards individuals for the single-minded pursuit of self-interest will face crises in its families.

Reordering the priorities of society in order to value children and families more highly is a major moral agenda for our time. No one segment of society can do it alone. The nuclear family by itself does not have the clout to demand what it needs in the face of economic pressures and political realities. The church, which has for centuries been an advocate for the family, has muted its public voice on the issue. The reordering of society to foster a family-friendly environment requires a spirit of collaboration between government, business corporations, churches, neighborhoods, and families themselves. At present, the level of trust is so low, the systems for blaming and powerlessness so entrenched in society and family alike, that cooperation and dialogue cannot be assumed even when the intent to aid the family is present.

The relatively recent resurgence of interest in the common good is a hopeful sign that we will find a way to reorder the priorities of society for the sake of children and families. It is not enough to expect that individual persons or particular families behave well. The structures of a society must be committed to creating an environment that fosters the common good, and must understand this as a commitment to pursue distributive and social justice. This emphasis on what is common does not eclipse individual particularity. Focus on the family need not, and should not, be at the expense of attending to the growing number of single households. The common good and competing individual claims must be in conversation because they implicate each other. Individuals, the family, and society will flourish only if there is an interactive network of institutions that seek to secure and enhance justice and human dignity for everyone.

The Restoration
of Neighborhoods

The commitment to the common good at the macrolevel is predicated on the existence of a parallel plan to develop neighborhoods at the local level. During the years these books have been written, it has come to be regarded as common wisdom that *it takes a village to raise a child*. Without a village, most everyone agrees, the family will fail. Families should not be blamed for failing to do what they never did alone. The threat to today's children is that the tribe no longer functions. Some people still live in villages or neighborhoods in which neighbors, shopkeepers, teachers, ministers, and other children's parents have a kind of covenant to work together, albeit informally, to raise their children. In all parts of our society, neighborhoods have disappeared behind fences and double-bolted doors amid gang warfare and the anonymity of urban living.

The restoration of neighborhoods is one way to make villages live again. Churches play a significant role in restoring neighborhoods. Churches have visions of the neighborhoods that fear and isolationism have removed. The formation of such visions is strengthened by conversations about the common good. However, the restoration of neighborhoods will not happen unless we learn how to live with and honor diversity. Many of those conversations in search of the common good for neighborhoods is complicated by the growing diversity in the communities in which we live. In situations that demand organized community advocacy to address basic needs, churches are in a position to bring people together to develop covenants of commitment that will respect difference and foster the common good. The future of family as well as the planet depends on learning how to live interdependently.

We may not yet be clear what the village should look like, but we are sure that we need to reshape society for the sake of children. Such a neighborhood will at least provide the kind of protection that fosters freedom for everyone, children and adults alike, to be vulnerable and needy as well as strong and self-sufficient. In order for the vision of the church to have the ring of authority, it must embody what it preaches and promotes. If the church intends to be a voice in neighborhoods and in the society for a new vision of living together in families, it must itself be a *sanctuary for childhood*. To be a sanctuary for childhood is to be a community where children are welcomed and honored as fully human and where there is compassion and justice for all persons.

The Family Is Both Public and Private

The idea that it takes a village to raise a child is only one instance of a larger and even more central theme for contemporary family living, one that has become increasingly clear to us: Marriage and the family are both a public and a private reality. When our deepest passions are aimed at preserving the nuclear family, we are sometimes intent on perpetuating a thinly disguised form of individualism and privatism. The privatization of the family (as an extension of American individualism) erodes an understanding of the interdependence of all things. This interdependence is illustrated by the awareness that the lives of single persons living alone are enriched by good marriages.

The process of becoming married includes a shift from a private promise to a public commitment. *Part of the church's role in prewedding preparation naturally attends to the public reality of marriage.* How a couple negotiates this transition from a private relationship to public status includes dimensions of both leaving their homes of origin and cleaving to one another to form a new bond. The marriage ritual is a public pledge, made between two people in the company of family and friends and in the presence of God, that they intend to become married. Although the work of becoming married is often done in private, and although it is important to preserve the privacy of a marital bond, marriage is a public reality as well.

If it takes a village to raise a child, it can also be said that it takes a village to stay married. A private marriage is an oxymoron. Every couple needs a public committed to enhance the well-being of a marriage. At one time, the extended family was public enough to provide that supportive context. Today, the ad hoc communities that gather for a wedding make promises to support this couple in their work of becoming and being married. Unfortunately, having made a public pledge of support, this company of family and friends retrieves its promise in order to honor the privacy of a couple. We do not mean to suggest that the wedding be understood as a blanket invitation to intrude on the marital privacy to make a marriage work. It is necessary, however, to reconsider the extent to which preoccupation with marital privacy has unwittingly made it more difficult to become and remain married by undermining the public character of marriage and family living. What is created and sustained in private is also maintained by the quality and form of public interaction by the marital pair.

Christian Themes for Family Living

In addition to asking what Scriptures and the Christian tradition have taught *about the family,* we need to begin to develop a theology *for the family* that draws on a wider range of resources from the tradition than specific teachings on or about the family. This distinction between a theology *of* the family and a theology *for* the family has been the methodological core of this series. The presence of two parents in an economically stable context will provide some idea about the resources that might be available to the family, but it does not tell us much about the family's ability to practice Christian virtues in their daily living. While it is important to explore what Christianity has taught specifically about the form and functions of family, a theology for the family is necessary in order to ask about general Christian virtues that are significant for family living, whatever the form or purpose.

A Christian vision for family living would include at least the following: (a) *The family is an hospitable community.* It welcomes the stranger, including the "stranger" who is each member of the family. The family's ability to be hospitable depends on having clear but permeable ways of separating the distinct units of any family system. (b) *The family is a compassionate community* because it cares for the most vulnerable ones. In order to be that kind of community, family members need to learn how to suffer with one another. (c) *The family is a just community* when all members, including children, are given equal respect, recognition, and consideration. (d) Because it is so difficult to hide our sinfulness in the family, *it is a community where forgiveness and reconciliation* are longed for and resisted but also offered and accepted again and again. These themes are not uniquely Christian but when filled with Christian meaning, they not only imply what is good enough; they form a vision of what the family could be.

The use of the term "family living" in the subtitle of this series has become more significant than we first intended. The focus on family living highlights the church's enduring contribution to the current family debate. Christian teaching has more to say about what families must do and how people must relate to one another than what families should look like. The vision of family living that has been developed in this series is not limited to one particular structure. It applies to families without children, single-parent families, and families of second marriages, as well as more traditional and extended nuclear families. It will be beneficial for the church to continue to identify the qualities of family living that honor the full humanity of children and the qualities of childhood in adults.

Over the last two centuries, family living has been less and less determined by external influences. Emotional bonding rather than social or economic imperatives are the primary normative source for internal family relations. As external control has decreased, the number of options for action within the family has increased. As a result, the modern family is threatened by inner, emotional disintegration. The return to greater external influence on the internal affairs of a family is not a desirable solution to the moral problems of family living today. Rather, the future of family depends on maintaining *a balance within itself between the claims for justice and needs for affection.*

The form of a family follows from it's function or purpose. For that reason it is important to be clear about the purpose of families. If, for example, child-rearing is the primary purpose of the family, then we must ask what forms will enable the family to fulfill that function. Because people live longer and have fewer children, the purpose of the family cannot be limited to child-rearing. The reality is that more married couples will spend at least half of their life together after the children have left home. The legitimate concern that family units maintain stability in order to provide a context for raising children does not address the issue of the marital bond when the nest is empty. The purposes of the family change over the life cycles of marriages or other committed relationships. So do the dynamics of the marital bond and the family as a system. In order to respond creatively to these ongoing changes, family members need to keep promising to one another again and again.

Change, Adaptation, and Family Grieving

From the beginning of this project, the intent has been to weave the framework of grief and the necessity of grieving with a systemic, life-cycle perspective on the family. The capacity to mourn is a key factor in family stability because families keep changing. In a sense, this emphasis on grief is a consequence of understanding change as an inevitable dimension of a family's history. Where there is change, there will be loss even when the change is hoped for and is mostly a gain. And where there is loss in human life, there will be grief. At the beginning we did not anticipate how central the motif of grieving would become in understanding transitions in family living over the life cycle.

It has only become clearer, as this series has evolved, that when a family cannot or does not mourn, it will get stuck in ways that are often problematic for individuals as well as the family as a whole. Ideally, families seek a balance between continuity and discontinuity. When the family's adaptation to a loss is rigid and inflexible in order to maximize continuity and minimize discontinuity, it often develops an intergenerational legacy that will make it difficult for subsequent generations to respond to loss. The ability to accept loss is at the heart of healthy family living. A family that grieves together will be more open to possibilities for growth. When a family cannot grieve, it gets stuck.

Grieving the loss is a response to change that looks to the past. There is another response to change that turns toward the future and understands change and adaptation as adventure. The family's courage to adapt makes it easier to live through change. This capacity to change in a deeper, more enduring sense is enhanced by the belief that the continuity of all creation, including the family, is in God. Paradoxically, families that accept change as inevitable and good will be more open to what God is making new. Transformation, as change beyond grieving and beyond adaptation, is necessary for the future of family living.

The Paradox of Family Living

Living the paradox is a central motif of life and faith. It is also foundational for family living. From the Christian perspective, to live the paradox as individuals and families is to walk the way of the cross, to know that life is gained in death. To walk the way of the cross is to live with contradictions that cannot be resolved. It is only by living the contradictions that we will participate in the power and hope of the cross. Change does not eliminate paradox. It remains even when change occurs. The aim of family living is therefore more than balance. It is the ability to live with the fundamental paradox of autonomy in community. *To be totally committed to the well-being of the family as community and totally committed to the development of each person in the family is as impossible as it is necessary.*

From a dynamic point of view, families are likely to get into trouble when they cannot accommodate the fundamental paradox of autonomy in community. Those who live alone always struggle between honoring individual opportunities and needs while at the same time reaching out to those relationships that will fulfill their created communal destiny. Becoming married requires a similar balance between community and individual autonomy, between self-determination and sacrifice, between private and public realities, and between continuity and discontinuity with one's past. Raising children is also rooted in paradox. Because our children are small and needy, we must protect and nurture them. Because they are a unique gift from God, we respect the story they will unfold. We are therefore both loving them and letting them go from the beginning of life. When the children leave home, this paradox takes new form as wives and husbands struggle to honor the new opportunities for freedom with what is required to maintain the marital bond.

The future of family depends in part on learning to live with paradox. In order to live paradoxically as individuals and as families, we need to avoid absolutizing alternatives. One can almost always say at least two things about anything, including family living, and both are true. God has placed the deepest and most fundamental contradictions in human life to be lived with in full awareness of their contradictoriness. The deeper truths of our lives need contradiction for full expression.

What is necessary for family living is also crucial for our conversations about the family. If we listen to the other side, we are more likely to discover a common agenda that supports both living alone and living in families, that honors children and strengthens families in all their forms, and that invites us to live in the promise that God continues to make all things new, even families. For the sake of the future of family, it is important to find ways of inviting conversation about family living that avoids polarizing the issue. We live the questions in hope that we will live into the answers. That is perhaps the most important thing we have learned from reflecting together at the end of this series.

Writing this epilogue was the catalyst for a lively and enlightening conversation among the people whose names appear at the end. We wish the same for you.

> Herbert Anderson
> Phyllis Anderson
> David Hogue
> Diane Stephens
> Freda Gardner
> Robert Cotton Fite
> Diane Hutchinson
> Susan B. W. Johnson
> Dennis Johnson
> Marie McCarthy, S.P.

NOTE: This epilogue may be duplicated for one-time use in discussion groups.

NOTES

Introduction

1. In the past twenty years, the number of men and women living alone has grown by more than 112 percent. Census figures have gone from 10,850,000 in 1970 to 23 million in 1975. Of those who live alone, 61 percent are women.

2. Herbert Anderson and Robert Cotton Fite, *Becoming Married* (Louisville, Ky.: Westminster/John Knox Press, 1993). A good marriage, according to Rainer Maria Rilke, is one in which each partner appoints the other "guardian of his solitude" (*Rilke on Love and Other Difficulties,* ed. John Mood [New York: W. W. Norton & Co., 1975], 28).

3. The following books focus more on being single than on living alone: Susan Annette Muto, *Celebrating the Single Life: A Spirituality for Single Persons in Today's World* (New York: Crossroad, 1981); Kay Collier Slone, *Singles in the Church* (Washington, D.C.: Alban Institute, 1992); William V. Arnold and Margaret Anne Fohl, *When You Are Alone* (Louisville, Ky.: Westminster/John Knox Press, 1990); John R. Landgraf, *Singling: A New Way to Live the Single Life* (Louisville, Ky.: Westminster/John Knox Press, 1990); Carolyn A. Koons and Michael J. Anthony, *Single Adult Passages: Uncharted Territories* (Grand Rapids: Baker Book House, 1991); Harold Ivan Smith, *Reluctantly Single: You Can Stop Waiting for Life to Happen and Start to Live* (Nashville: Abingdon Press, 1994).

4. Carol M. Anderson and Susan Stewart, with Sonia Dimidjian, *Flying Solo: Single Women in Midlife* (New York: W. W. Norton & Co., 1994). "Models of single women who have successfully negotiated a place for themselves in this new world, who have learned how to fly solo, are essential for all women struggling to make it on their own. Positive models of single women could also have a profound impact on women who may never be single. Women are more likely to find satisfaction in their intimate relationships if they do not feel desperate about them" (16). We would say the same about the theme of living alone.

5. Charles Handy, *The Age of Paradox* (Boston: Harvard Business School Press, 1994), 13.

6. Raymond Belliotti, *Seeking Identity: Individualism Versus Community in an Ethnic Context* (Lawrence: University of Kansas Press, 1995), 38.

7. Ibid., 37.

8. Martin E. Marty, *Friendship* (Allen, Tex.: Argus Communications, 1980), 11.

Chapter 1. Living Alone, Being Whole

1. Letty Russell, *Becoming Human* (Philadelphia: Westminster Press, 1982), 64.

2. Frances K. Goldscheider and Calvin Goldscheider, *Leaving Home before Marriage* (Madison: University of Wisconsin Press, 1993), 113.

3. Richard A. Shweder, *Thinking through Cultures: Expeditions in Cultural Psychology* (Cambridge, Mass.: Harvard University Press, 1991), 28.

4. Ibid., 102.

5. David Augsburger, *Pastoral Counseling across Cultures* (Philadelphia: Westminster Press, 1986), 102.

6. Phyllis Trible, *God and the Rhetoric of Sexuality* (Philadelphia: Fortress Press, 1978), 90.

7. Dianne Bergant and Carroll Stuhlmueller, "Creation according to the Old Testament," in *Evolution and Creation,* ed. Ernan McMullin (South Bend, Ind.: University of Notre Dame Press, 1985), 157.

8. Ibid., 158.

9. Russell, *Becoming Human,* 66–67.

10. Karl Barth, *Church Dogmatics,* vol. III/4 (Edinburgh: T. & T. Clark), 117.

11. John R. Sachs, S.J., *The Christian View of Humanity* (Collegeville, Minn.: Liturgical Press, 1991), 37.

12. Ibid.

13. Sallie McFague, *Models of God: Theology for an Ecological Nuclear Age* (Philadelphia: Fortress Press, 1987).

14. Ibid., 183.

Chapter 2. Living Alone after Living with Someone

1. Ginny Sprang and John McNeil, *The Many Faces of Bereavement* (New York: Brunner/Mazel Publishers, 1995), 3.

2. Colin Murray Parkes and Robert S. Weiss, *Recovery from Bereavement* (New York: Basic Books, 1983), 111.

3. Ibid., 243.

4. Sprang and McNeil, 182.

5. Froma Walsh and Monica McGoldrick, *Living Beyond Loss: Death in the Family* (New York: W. W. Norton & Co., 1991).

6. Froma Walsh and Monica McGoldrick, "Loss and the Family Life Cycle," in *Family Transitions,* ed. Celia Jaes Falicov (New York: Guilford Press, 1988), 314.

7. Ibid., 315.

8. Ibid., 328.

9. Ibid.

10. Jane Burgess Kohn and Willard K. Kohn, *The Widower* (Boston: Beacon Press, 1978), 95.

11. Thomas Attig, *How We Grieve: Relearning the World* (New York: Oxford University Press, 1996), 107–8.

12. Beverley Raphael, *The Anatomy of Bereavement* (New York: Basic Books, 1983), 209.

13. R. Scott Sullender, *Losses in Later Life: A New Way of Walking with God* (Mahwah, N.J.: Paulist Press, 1989), 121.

14. Ibid., 118.

15. Ibid., 119.

Chapter 3. Always Living Alone

1. Don Browning, "The Family and the Male Problematic," *Dialog* 34, no. 2 (spring 1995): 123–130.

2. Natalie Schwartzberg, Kathy Berliner, and Demaris Jacod, *Single in a Married World: A Life Cycle Framework for Working with the Unmarried Adult* (New York: W. W. Norton & Co. 1994), 26–27.

3. Judith Viorst, *Necessary Losses* (New York: Simon & Schuster, 1986), 39.

4. Ted Bowman, *Loss of Dreams: A Special Kind of Grief* (published by the author, 2111 Knapp Street, St. Paul, Minnesota, 1994).

5. There are many books similar to Bernard Siegel's *Love, Medicine and Miracles* (New York: Harper & Row, Harper Perennial books, 1986) that offer useful strategies for taking control of one's life under a variety of stressful conditions.

6. Reynolds Price, *A Whole New Life* (New York: Atheneum Publishers, 1994), 182f.

Chapter 4. Special Situations of Living Alone

1. Agnes Farris, "Commuting," in *Working Couples,* ed. Robert and Rhona Rapoport (New York: Harper & Row, 1978), 107.

2. Paul Tillich, *The Shaking of the Foundations* (New York: Charles Scribner's Sons, 1948), 149.

3. Ibid., 154. For further exploration of the theological significance of waiting, see W. H. Vanstone, *The Stature of Waiting* (London: Darton, Longman & Todd, 1982). For Vanstone, "waiting can be the most intense and poignant of all human experiences—the experience which, above all all others, strips us of affectation and self-deception, and reveals to us the reality of our needs, our values and ourselves" (83).

4. John S. Dunne, "Insight and Waiting on God," in *Creativity and Method: Essays in Honor of Bernard Lonergan,* ed. Matthew L. Lamb (Milwaukee: Marquette University Press, 1981).

Chapter 5. Alternatives to Loneliness: Solitude and Friendship

1. In preliterate societies, older persons not only maintained socially important roles and positions of power, it was expected that they would be cared for within the kinship network. George L. Maddox, "The Social and Cultural Context of Aging," in *Aging: The Process and the People,* ed. Gene Usdin, M.D., and Charles K. Hofling, M.D. (New York: Brunner/Mazel Publishers, 1978), 20–46.

2. Philip Slater, *The Pursuit of Loneliness* (Boston: Beacon Press, 1970), xii.

3. Louise Bernikow, *Alone in America: The Search for Companionship* (New York: Harper & Row, 1986), 12.

4. Robert E. Neale, *Loneliness, Solitude, and Companionship* (Philadelphia: Westminster Press, 1984), 48.

5. William Wordsworth, "The Prelude." *William Wordsworth: A Critical Edition of the Major Works*, ed. Stephen Gill (New York: Oxford University Press, 1984).

6. Henri J. M. Nouwen, *Reaching Out: The Three Movements of the Spiritual Life* (Garden City, N.Y.: Doubleday & Co. 1975), 25.

7. Thomas Merton, *Thoughts in Solitude* (New York: Farrar, Straus & Cudahy, 1956, 1958), 58. For an exploration of the theme of solitude in relation to the creative life, see Anthony Storr, *Solitude: A Return to the Self* (New York: Ballantine Books, 1988). "Perhaps the need of the creative person for solitude, and his preoccupation with internal processes of integration, can reveal something about the needs of the less gifted, more ordinary human being which is, at the time of writing, neglected" (xv).

8. Neale, *Loneliness, Solitude, and Companionship,* 58.

9. May Sarton, *Journal of a Solitude* (New York: W. W. Norton & Co., 1992), 87, 11.

10. Neale, *Loneliness, Solitude, and Companionship,* 87.

11. Merton, *Thoughts in Solitude,* 85.

12. Ibid., 113.

13. Ibid., 117.

14. Neale, *Loneliness, Solitude, and Companionship,* 115.

15. Marty, *Friendship,* 7.

16. McFague, *Models of God,* 167. God's relationship with humankind, after the model of solidarity friendship, is that "we do not belong to ourselves, but it also says we are not left to ourselves" (167).

17. Compare with Eudora Welty and Ronald A. Sharp, eds., *The Norton Book of Friendship* (New York: W. W. Norton & Co., 1991).

18. Nouwen, *Reaching Out,* especially pages 14–44 for his discussion of the movement from loneliness to solitude. "Friendship and community are, first of all, inner qualities allowing human togetherness to be the playful expression of a much larger reality. . . . This inner sense of friendship and community sets us free to live a 'worldly' life even in the seclusion of a room, since no one should be excluded from our solitude" (33).

19. Dietrich Bonhoeffer, *Prayers from Prison* (London: William Collins Sons & Co., 1977), 29. This poem on friendship was addressed by Bonhoeffer to a particular friend, Eberhard Bethge. In his commentary on the poem, Johann Christoph Hampe emphasizes the connection between freedom and friendship, intensified by the fact that Bonhoeffer wrote the poem in prison. "It is the nature of friendship that it grows in freedom, unprotected and 'in glad confidence.'" (74–75).

20. McFague, *Models of God,* 20.

21. Gilbert C. Meilaender, *Friendship: A Study in Theological Ethics* (Notre Dame, Ind.: University of Notre Dame Press, 1981), 66.

22. Paul Wadell, C.P., "The Role of Friendship in the Moral and Spiritual Development of Seminarians," in *Seminary Journal* 1, no. 2 (fall 1995): 28. For further reading on Paul Wadell's views on friendship, see *Friendship and the Moral Life* (Notre Dame, Ind.: University of Notre Dame Press, 1989).

23. Ibid., 21.

Chapter 6. Alone with Others in Church

1. The hidden or null curriculum is that which we exclude for one reason or another thereby eliminating the possibility that we might learn from it. For a discussion of this idea, see Elliot Eisner, *The Educational Imagination* (New York: Macmillan Publishing Co., 1979) and Maria Harris, *Fashion Me a People* (Louisville, Ky.: Westminster/John Knox Press, 1989).

2. Carl E. Braaten and Robert W. Jensen, eds., *Christian Dogmatics*, vol. 2 (Philadelphia: Fortress Press, 1984), 223–241.

3. John Calvin, *Institutes of the Christian Religion*, trans. Ford Lewis Battles, ed. John T. McNeill (Philadelphia: Westminster Press, 1960), 4.1.9: "We have laid down as distinguishing marks of the Church the preaching of the Word and the observance of the sacraments. These can never exist without bringing forth fruit and prospering by God's blessing" (p. 1024).

4. We are indebted to John Linnan, C.S.V., for his generous assistance in developing this chapter.

5. Philip Hefner, "The Community of Possibility: Belonging without Conditions" (unpublished manuscript).

6. Rebecca Chopp, "In the Real World: A Feminist Theology for the Church," *Quarterly Review* 16, no. 1 (spring 1996): 3–22.

7. Gerald Foley, *Family-Centered Church: A New Parish Model,* (Kansas City: Sheed & Ward, 1995), 17.

8. Sallie McFague, *Metaphorical Theology: Models of God in Religious Language* (Philadelphia: Fortress Press, 1982), 180. Our approach to the church as a "community of friends" has also been influenced by Celia Allison Hahn (*Sexual Paradox* [Cleveland: Pilgrim Press, 1991]).

9. Chopp, "In the Real World," 15. Mary Frohlich has written about the theological significance of sexuality in a way that brings together many of the themes of this book. Sexuality, she suggests, is the orientation of the human person towards communion with other human persons and with God. "Theologically, the most radical fulfilment of this communion is articulated in terms of mystical communion and Church. *All human beings, regardless of sex, gender identity, marital status, or any other conjugate of human being, are called to the gift of this communion within human friendship, life in a community of disciples, and mystical communion with God*" (italics added). Human beings are destined for community, and the church is an inclusive reality. "From Mystification to Mystery: Lonergan and the Theological Significance of Sexuality," in *Lonergan and Feminism,* ed. Cynthia S. W. Crysdale (Toronto: University of Toronto Press, 1994), 190.